Refugees and

Peacekeepers

Refugees a

Peacekeep

A Patrician Press A

Patrician Press

Manningtree

First published as a paperback edition by Patrician Press 2017

E-book edition published by Patrician Press 2017

Copyright © Patrician Press 2017

British Library Cataloguing in Publication Data. A catalogue record for this book is available from the British Library.

ISBN paperback edition 978-0-9934945-6-7

ISBN e-book edition 978-0-9934945-4-3

First published by Patrician Press in 2017

For more information: www.patricianpress.com

"I felt a terrible pity and kind of anger that it should be like this. It wasn't just the sight of them, it was reading the rhetoric against them. They were being described essentially as hate objects, they were all potential terrorists, they were all potential scroungers, we shouldn't do anything for them, we should in a sense keep them out" George Szirtes

(After seeing refugees camped in Keleti railway station in Budapest.)

"I appeal to ministers to look into their hearts and take immediate action to bring these children to safety. It has been established that the UK has a legal obligation to these children, but more to the point, this country has a moral obligation" The Bishop of Barking

(On seeing the refugee children trapped in the Calais 'Jungle Camp'.)

Contents

Introduction by Anna Johnson

Human beings use the written word to map the visible world around them. We have a substantial linguistic toolbox at our disposal—many alphabets to express many subtleties. So it is striking that in recent times, words have become hard-edged and dangerous. Political figures across the world are reaching for words that seek to accuse, to isolate and most of all, to frighten. And fear isn't subtle.

The images of a drowned toddler washed up on a Turkish beach last September prompted outrage and grief: an innocent life cut brutally short, words seemed inadequate. The British government was forced to increase its resettlement quota and there was not a shadow of doubt that everyone felt that this was the very least we could do. So it seems odd that a little over a year later in 2016, the British people seem so much less amenable to the idea of people taking refuge on these shores. The dispossessed and displaced are still fleeing across land and sea, but our view of them has undergone a seachange. There has been a collective intake of breath in response to a narrative of intolerance. Many now believe that there isn't enough on our small island to go around. Now the boundaries that divide us are potent symbols: the world over there is for you, the world over here is for us. There can be no grey areas.

Except that human existence is all about the grey areas—and it is those that this new anthology explores—providing a space for stories to be told and voices to be heard. Hence the Patrician Press's first writing competition held earlier this year (2016) entitled: Refugees and Peacekeepers. The winners' responses, and those of established Patrician writers aim to use the power of writing to break down the barriers to empathy and show how every human life should be valued.

Twenty-four writers, then, have taken up the challenge of elucidating the margins. Indeed, the anthology closes with a clarion call from Ian Shaw, musician and volunteer, on his experiences in that most notorious of grey areas—the *jungle* in Calais—or, as he describes it: 'a lawless, yet often stimulating microcosm of all our funny old worlds.'

Some writers consider the experiences of people on their migration, others their experiences of living as a migrant in a foreign country. *The Milk* by Naomi Hamill, is a story about the kindness that is sometimes shown when even the giver has little more than a cow and four walls to share. Conversely, *The Boy on the Beach* by Susan Pope takes a bleak look at people trafficking, wherein a child is reduced to, 'a piece of luggage folded and creased.' For Ania in *Leavings* by Petra McQueen, a postcard that reminds her of home throws into sharp relief the dreary half-life she is living far from her son and all that she values. Katherine Blessan's story is an inter-generational testament of endurance—can any of us remain unmoved by the mixture of love and desperate hope behind the resolve to travel by wheelchair across whole countries?

Two stories focus on what it is like to feel trapped and to yearn for a new beginning. In *Running through New York* by Priya Guns, the sensual vibrancy of the locality contrasts with the reality of weevils in the international aid parcels, but the protagonist's daydreams cannot ultimately mask a shocking truth. Nesreen Salem, meanwhile, evokes the purgatorial transit zone between arriving and leaving—the 'place of infinite space and time,' that is *Limbo*.

You, Sameh by Kathy Stevens explores the perspective of a woman who has chosen to give a home to a refugee girl. Using spare, unflinching prose, she makes clear that loneliness can make us refugees in our own lives—misery makes our narrator diffident and cold. But this is a message of hope and inclusivity: here it is the outsider who unites and heals.

The winner of our short story prize is *Winter Solstice* by Penny Simpson. It is a narrative that is alive to its connections with the seasons and the passage of time—a celebration of cultural differences and shared humanity. Two very different characters find strength in each other during a single solstice night—the long dark is filled with colour and light, memory and miracle.

An anthology theme is not, of course, a rigid demand. To wit, *Milanese Feast* by Emma Kittle-Pey, in which the narrator, by turns amused and exasperated, curious and sympathetic, eavesdrops during a hotel breakfast—and resolves to keep the peace. *Brilliant Disguise* by Robert Ronsson has a rather different first person narrator, who points out, 'You don't know me, 'cos I don't exist.' Here is a man who has learned how to make himself invisible, so when by extraordinary luck he survives the catastrophe of 9/ 11, he becomes visible in a way that neither he nor the reader expects. Equally unexpected, perhaps, is a car which tells its own story: *Sunny the Indian Datsun* by Wersha Bharadwa is a parable of racial integration, by turns funny, moving and shrewd, and with a central character so endearing that it seems a shame that cars can't talk. *The Candidate* by Elisa Marcella Webb—set in the US—is an elegant illustration of what a difference a generation can make to the opportunities available to the 'help'.

Eleven of the writers in this volume have contributed poems which share with the prose an interest in the edges of things—society, countries, shorelines. In this poetry the texture of light and dark that informs this anthology is distilled.

Refuge is a Taxi by Pen Avey, focuses on the cabbie we barely pay heed to, seeing the potential in every migrant to be embraced and celebrated. *The Photo* by Aoife Lyall is an elegy for the small boy behind the image I alluded to earlier whose face—tragically—is *not* 'turned, coy, as though in sleep.' Mark Brayley's hypnotic but chilling lipogram, pens the general's daughter in her ivory tower, where she will never learn how her homeland has 'shuddered/under her father's hand.' In *Something Human*, Rebecca Balfourth urges a cross-border approach to charity for those who have never been 'bordered in and boarded up.' Other works examine how loss is compounded by an inability to understand the nuances of language (*The Lake* by Catherine Coldstream) or how hope can manifest itself in a 'Turner sunset' (*Evensong* by Louise G. Cole). Suzy Norman focuses on the devastation politely wreaked by bureaucracy and on the significance of prints in snow. There is a reminder of the exotic in *Nina and the Rain* by Kenneth Stevens as a counterpoint to the darker musings about the breakdown of the human spirit when it sees, 'no way forward... no way back' (*The Border* by Susannah Tassell). In *Émigré*, Anna Vaught makes the point that, 'we are all from an island or a foreign sun,' all a 'part of the main'—there is indeed no such thing as difference in a world where we all go back to 'uncertain dust.'

We are all looking for significance in life—to be significant to our family, our friends, our God(s); it seems that the particular tragedy of refugees—unwanted as they are—is to become literally effaced. As a mass movement, they lose individuality. Hopefully, one of the things this anthology achieves is to give faces to those in the crowd—to restore some humanity, some significance and some love.

Editor's postscript: As this edition is reprinted, Amber Rudd has announced the 'winding-up' of the Dubs Amendment, with only 350 out of an intended 3000 lone child refugees likely to reach our shores. The Archbishop of Canterbury summed up the mood when he said, 'We must resist and turn back the worrying trends... towards seeing the movement of desperate people as more of a threat to identity and security than an opportunity to do our duty.'

Into the void, in the unregulated camps springing up again around Calais, unprotected children are easy prey for hovering traffickers.

How quickly we forget, how shamefully we sully our long tradition of offering sanctuary to the most vulnerable.

Anna Johnson, editor

Refuge is a Taxi by Pen Avey

A city gent gets into Basim's taxi cab.

Speaks on his mobile—never misses a beat.

A Rolex peeks from beneath

His gold-cufflinked Paul Smith shirt.

The fare comes to ten pounds

And a tenner is tendered.

Still, Basim smiles and wishes

His customer a nice evening.

Later that night two girls

Giggle behind freshly hennaed hands.

They speak of boys they like

Boldly in Urdu; never guessing

That their lowly driver speaks eleven languages—five fluently.

They tip him two pounds.

He could say goodbye in their mother tongue

But he is far too polite.

Between jobs Basim studies.

He wants to learn how to fix cars,

To own his own garage, maybe. One day

He wishes to get married, start a family.

His hopes are simple, yet complex,

But dreaming is enough to spur him on.

He has come this far—there is no edge

To this land of opportunity.

Yet in the dark they come again

To wrap his hands around the

Cold, hard barrel of an assault rifle.

Sweat stings his eyes, and he wipes it away

As he watches out for the enemy.

His friend is shot through the cheek—

Ragged flesh exposing teeth

As a wasted life ebbs away.

Basim runs, his heart thumps,

Rasping breath, blood in his throat.

He hides a while in the bleak mountains.

He weeps, he prays.

He wakes—the holy words still on his lips,

Thanking Allah for answered prayers.

Removing the sweat-soaked pillow slip to air,

Basim hums as he heads outside,

For the freedom of his next fare.

Something Human by Rebecca Balfourth

They say charity starts at home.
They say home's where the heart is
and I find my heart can cross borders
to sprawl on the couch of a person
I've never known.
By virtue of a red passport,
I've grown in places not my own,
had the privilege to call them home
and left my heart lying around
casual, careless.
I can't imagine what it's like to be
placeless, faceless, nameless,
a story in another place's papers.
To be bordered in and boarded up—
I've never pleaded with strangers
to let me in to a cold and foreign nation
where I feel unwelcome,
derided and despised for trying

to save my life.
I've never fled.
I've never seen one person dead
at the hands of another.
Whatsoever you do to the least of my brothers,
that you do unto me
and I can believe that's true.
So if charity starts at home,
and if home's where the heart is,
my heart goes out to strangers
like a note in a bottle, its message
something human
something strong.

Sunny the Indian Datsun
by Wersha Bharadwa

8am, 21 May 1989, 8am

I was born in Japan to Japanese parents. But I'm not Japanese.
I'm English. Look at my number plate. Or ask Stuart, my last
owner. Huh. There's that lump in my exhaust pipe again. I
can't talk about him these days without welling up. At first I
was a bit wary of the shaven head and tattoos but Sunny Blue
told me I was lucky to be snapped up by a white person at
least.

Most of the other Datsuns, he warned back then, are
getting bought left, right and centre by Asian families. 'Have
you ever pulled up next to Indians at a traffic light?' he said as
I got ready to leave the first time. 'I saw six adults in the back
of Sunny Old, two kids lying across his backseat floor with
everyone using them as footstools and two heads and tails
across laps as blankets. And that's not forgetting the 15-year-
old using the gearstick as a surf board.' I shuddered at the
vision. Sunny Blue was getting on my fucking nerves with

his constant renditions of 'Tomorrow' from Annie while he waited for someone to give his busted-up, old-banger body a home. I felt being owned by someone like Stuart meant settling for too little, but turns out I loved my life with him. Besides, who can afford to be picky?

Then he got sent down. 'Winson Green, FUCKING, Winson Green,' he'd cried repeatedly in my front mirror three weeks ago. He groaned before feebly whispering: 'Promise you'll do a drive by visit.' I swiped my windscreen wipers left to say 'yes'. He knew it'd be a difficult time for me, so he replaced my car manual with his treasured copy of *Mein Kampf* and a tin of Spam and put a stylish Swastika sticker inside my glove compartment just as the flashing sirens came for him. 'Yaw keep 'em safe foduh pigs,' he said.

So here I am, Sunny Silver, back at the dealership. 'Stuart was a thug,' Sunny Black said, as he tried to console me. I always fought back: 'He was everything to me.' Because he was. He was my family. He'd left the National Front three years ago to join this exciting new splinter group, The British National Party. He and his friends had grown tired of the politics. They just wanted to have fun, beat guys up. He even gave me a sticker on my bumper! It was such a moment. Now Stuart's holed up in the brownest prison in Christendom.

The showroom owner takes my 'For Sale' sign off. He pats my bonnet and tells me I'm now a royal carriage for a family of unsavoury foreigners who've paid over the odds for me. Stuart reckons this new influx are the worst immigrants we've ever had. Says they're the reason his brothers are signing on—they're taking all the jobs. I can't believe this is going to be my life now. It's a nightmare.

12pm

I'm being driven very carefully by a man with a big handlebar moustache, wearing strong cologne. He'd spoken to the garage owner a few moments ago. 'Two grandparents, two parents and three children,' he said. 'The perfect model for youse Indians!' the garage owner said. 'He-yaare, yaw'll easily get the cousins in taw!' They both laughed. I was horrified. If I had a religion, I'd be praying now. Stuart and his friends talked about how Indians ate beetles and drank blood after watching Indiana Jones and The Temple of Doom. 'Watch the film and get clued up!' he yelled at one pub rally. 'They eat chilled monkey brains for fuck's sake!'

I think the man senses my horror—I've only five seats! So he gently strokes my dashboard and smiles in my mirror. 'Life is good,' he says to himself—or maybe me—triumphantly. I'm supposed to be the most reliable vehicle ever, but now... I doubt I'll last long.

12.15pm

I feel the water drain from my engine face as I pull up next to Sunny Black at the Stratford Road and Robin Hood Lane traffic lights. He's in absolute stitches, alternating between stalling himself on purpose and rip-revving. His new clueless owner swears across the wheel but I know Sunny's wetting himself over the little statue of an Elephant god now dangling from my mirror. Fucker. He's remembering my story about Stuart always telling his boys to display their Union Jacks in the same spot. I pretend it doesn't bother me and I'm okay until we get to the new owner's house. A woman comes to take a look at me. 'Your own car, Ashok!'

she beams at him. He's undeniably chuffed. 'To go with the house,' he smiles. 'No more buses or landlords.'

As the man makes his way out of the drive into the house, the woman finds the book, tin of Spam and swastika sticker Stuart placed inside the glove compartment. 'Ashok! Ashok!' she screams. Come quickly! It's a sign! A Hindu car with a Saathiyo sign. God has blessed us for our troubles!'

'Er... That's not a Saathiyo, dear,' he replies. 'Where're the dots? And it's back to front... That's Hitler's bastard swastika! This car is racialist! Last owner must've been BNP. Bastards!'

The woman rushes into the house and comes back with a silver steel tray with some red food powder colouring on it and a small bowl of water, rice and green lentils. What the fuck's she going to do? Cook over my water engine? This is the exact devil-worshipping Stuart spoke about. 'Tina! Neal! Sunny!' the woman yells loudly. Three kids rush out of the semi-detached. 'Look Sunny! Daddy's new car has your name!'

The boy, who's around five, shoots his siblings a look as their mother jumps into the passenger seat with her devil tray. He begins chanting theatrically:

Kali maa! Shakti De!
Kali Maa! Shakti De!

The other two join in, swaying terrifyingly from side to side, chanting:

Mola Ram,
Seedaram,
Mola Ram Seedaram

I've never been so scared in my life. They're actually doing the chant from Indiana Jones. Stuart was right all along. I have got to escap—

'Shut up, you idiots,' the man, Ashok, cuts in.

'They don't even bloody know who Kalika Maa is, Sarita. They watch Indiana bloody Jones all day and get excited because the actors are Indian. You need to send them to Gujarati school.'

The children fall about laughing in hysterics before their mother urges them to watch what she's doing. She peels off my sticker, turns it around, paints over the black with the red paste and puts dots everywhere.

'There... a saathiyo... blessed,' she says.

Ashok hands her the tin of Spam.

'You want me to spice this up at my brother's over the weekend?'

I think she's talking about making Spam curry. It sounds worse than chilled monkey brains.

8pm

They all pile inside me. The teenage daughter, Tina, is fighting with the mother because her nails are stained from the turmeric in her dinner. Ashok snaps and reminds Sarita to book Gujarati school places ASAP so the kids don't lose their culture. Neal, the eldest son, says he doesn't need to go. Says he knows all about Kali Maa from Indiana Jones and the Temple of Doom and she scares the shit out of him. Tina punches him in the chest for swearing, then gets shouted at by Sarita for daring to hit her son. I get the feeling he's a big deal but I'm reaching my limits.

'That film you love, it's racialist to Indians,' says Ashok as he drives.

'But you love it too,' Tina, protests.

'Roshan Seth was on top of the world after he played Nehru,' says Ashok. 'Then they knock him back down by making him play an evil Indian blood-drinking savage in his very next English film. It's sacrilege.'

'A job's a job,' says Sarita. 'But Roshan's mistake was not addressing accuracy. He should've said: "Spielberg, why you making Kalika the baddie? I'll give you 50 demons from the ancient texts."'

Sarita talks about a co-worker complaining about her bringing Indian food to the office for lunch, working all hours and being served last at the local supermarket. But instead of telling the woman to pipe down and be grateful they have jobs, unlike Stuart's brothers, Ashok says: 'We don't protest verbally. You go buy from our own shops.' It's exactly what Stuart said they'd do! Take over the economy! It's a nightmare. There Stuart was trying to send them all back, here I am with them in the back. I'll drive by Winson Green tomorrow.

26 May 1989

I'm feeling bad about locking the interior door on the passenger seat and making Sarita scramble across the handbrake in her sari. Why do they wear those things? It's not ancient Greece anymore! We have Singer machines!! I know this because Stuart's friends stole a load and stashed them on my back seat, which is why I have the small tear in my stitching. Maybe I had to be sold to brown people as karma for being an accessory in handling stolen goods. Or when I was a getaway car for Stuart after he beat the West

Indian kid. *Oh God.* Whatever you do, don't tell Ashok and Sarita I said that word. Karma. They're totally obsessed by it.

3 July 1989

I'm taking the grandparents to the airport. They call India the 'Motherland' but none of them has ever set foot in the country. Even I don't call Japan the Motherland and I was born there. They hate the British rain. Perhaps we have something in common after all. Ashok, who drives an awful lot, says they better get used to it because a man called Idi Amin isn't inviting them for a *jamvanu* any time soon. I think it means feast—they go to a lot of *jamvanus*.

And I think they had to leave Uganda quickly; that Idi fellow was threatening to put them in concentration camps. The grandparents tell the children how they had their gold and money robbed by soldiers at gun point as they boarded the plane here. Maybe they didn't come here to steal jobs like Stuart thought after all.

29 July 1989

Tina thinks Soul II Soul's 'Back 2 Life' has the answers to life's pressing questions. When she isn't forcefully jamming an illegally recorded cassette into the mouth of my stereo player, she's permanently attached to her Walkman. Ashok asks her to share his love for this singer called Kishore Kumar—who is growing on me each day, by the way—but she refuses. Calls it embarrassing. She's wrong. Her addiction to Kylie is.

Sarita announces she wants to visit the Motherland before she dies.

'I'm never going to India—ever!' cries Sunny. 'They drink blood in the temple of Kali!'

Ashok tenses up. He accelerates harder. 'See? See the bullshit our kids are coming up with over their history? Sunny, Indians in India are mostly vegetarians.'

'I'm not,' Tina swipes back, 'I eat hamburger happy meals.'

'Oh ham is fine,' replies Sarita. 'It's not really even meat.'

'They drink blood!' Sunny protests again.

'It's true,' says Tina. 'They don't just make up things as big as that about Indians from nowhere.'

'They do in Hollywood,' Ashok says. 'They get paid for it too.'

1 December 1989

I'm still unsure what to make of Ashok's stories. They compel and repel me. I try to shuffle my memories of happier times with Stuart, but this chatty man with his loud-as-fuck family, they don't let me do anything but be fascinated. Like, did you know they speak three languages? English, Swahili and Gujarati? They were landowners in Africa, had businesses and servants. Ashok was a medical student. 'Now I have to smile sweetly at colleagues who talk about going to the 'paki shop' for cigarettes as we buy rounds at the pub,' he reminds Sarita today. She touches his face. 'Not in front of the kids,' she says.

We're en route to Leicester again this evening. I always know because the kids are made to sit on massive duvets and pillows in the back and there's talk of how the men will drink and sleep on kitchen floors. Ashok always plays Kishore Kumar and talks of Africa and his job at British Gas on long drives.

Sarita's boss has banned her home-made lunches. '*No Indian or strong-smelling food allowed*, there was a sign on the fridge,' she cries. Ashok puts his hand on her thigh. 'Give it five years, darling,' he says. 'When Tesco start making saag paneer ready meals, *every office* will smell of curry. Watch.' But Sarita can't shift her sadness. 'I can't win,' she says. 'I'm not good enough for the satsang group because my Indian singing accent has a hint of Queen's English from boarding school and I'm a non-white person called Rita at work. And my hair stinks of wee because Sunny refuses to control his bladder or leave our bed at SEVEN.'

Sunny's thing is still quoting lines from *Indiana Jones* and The Temple of Doom. Whenever he's in trouble, his response is always the same: 'The stones will be found, Dr Jones, you won't! You won't! HAHAHAHAHAHAHA.' Unusually, this cheers everybody up and they laugh. I do too.

5 January 1990

Sarita's midwife appointment at the Queen Elizabeth Hospital went well, she says when we pick her up. Ashok says he likes the Queen but not the lady running the country. I don't feel the urge to correct him like I did in the early days. In fact, I got really mad at Stuart's Dad when we passed him in the street the other day and he randomly shouted: 'Go back where you came from!' at the car, and when Ashok shouted: 'Fuck off you fat Racialist Bastard,' back at him I felt strangely satisfied.

5 May 1990

Sarita had a girl! I'm parked outside the maternity ward at Q.E Hospital. I want to share the news with everyone—Sunny Black, Sunny Red, even Sunny Old and Stuart!—I've never felt so happy. There's no one I know in the car park. Just as I choke up, Ashok opens the door and sits in the driver's seat. He looks in the mirror and pats my steering wheel. 'Congrats Sunny, you have another girl to carry home.' And suddenly I get it.

10 May 1990

Since bringing the baby back from the hospital, I've not been driven much. Ashok sits inside and has these weird cry-out sessions at the wheel. Relatives come and go at the house with huge gifts and the men come inside the car for a cheeky tot of whisky and a cigarette with Ashok. He offers them all the same lame joke: 'She's carrying out her two week confinement—but so am I!' I wonder how Sarita is. The car doesn't smell good without her.

27 March 1993

We pass Sparkbrook. Most Gujaratis have moved to Shirley and there's a big Mirpuri community here now. Ashok says the English people have a problem when immigrants don't make an effort to integrate—the way some of these families in their closed communities don't. Sarita raises her eyebrow. 'You're not better than anyone because you weren't born in a village, Ashok.'

'But that guy, he's throwing rubbish on the street!'

When I gasp (by letting the air out of my front tyre) Ashok knows I'm disgusted at him too. Somewhere on his journey, he's entered the weird British class system and found himself seated a little higher than uneducated brown people. My bonnet opens to speak but he runs outside and shuts it quickly. Ashok sighs at the sight of himself in my side mirror.

21 May 1993

Once a year they do a little Indian thanksgiving ceremony for me on my birthday. The stereo gets cranked up to full volume and they wash me and all the little statues inside my glove compartment. I get taken somewhere nice. It's not always Leicester. Baby Jayna is now three! She's addicted to saying 'poo-poo'. It's really cute.

14 December 1993

Sarita's driving more these days. She parks up and sees three aunties stood sniping in the dip of the pavement. One calls her a coconut. It makes Sarita cry. I don't think this is a bad term but it seems to affects her more than when she gets called a dirty p-word whenever she drives through Chelmsley Wood. 'Ashok, is it because my work means I'm hardly in sarees these days and not pulling my weight at Mandir committee meetings?' she asks.

'Who knows? Could be you spending time with non-

Asian friends or anglicising your name to Rita, or the kids speaking rubbish Gujurati.'

'I can't win,' she says. It's a sad day.

15 December 1993

Ashok hugs Sarita in the car. 'Let's go to the temple, shall we?'

He pats my steering wheel. 'Sunny, you're as loyal as a blind person's dog. Obviously you did something wrong to be reborn as a car, but you'll be a Labrador in the next life, *guaranteed*. You have good karma.'

6 August 1994

I am being dropped back at the dealership. Ashok has a new job—it's Mercedes time. The other Sunnys will be shocked—I ought to be at the scrap heap. Instead I look as good as the day I left. The family took care of me. Sarita is crying buckets and asking neighbours to pose in photos with the family standing next to me in the street. Ashok and I have a quiet moment when he hands back my key to the showroom owner. We're not the same as we were when we met. No one ever is, right? That's the thing about family. It always changes. And you change with it.

Travels by Wheelchair by Katherine Blessan

I told him that he should have left me behind. What use am I to him or to anyone for that matter? He told me that I was worth more than the whole Afghan army and Taliban put together, and he meant it. That gave me a sweet sensation like the taste of sheer payra fudge, reminding me that I am strong and sure at my core despite my age.

Abdul passes on to me whatever painkillers he is able to get hold of en route to mollify the constant pain that bites and claws around my spine. He is such a good boy, one of the best, like my Hamed (To Allah we belong and to Him is our return). But it seems that no matter how many painkillers he gets hold of, it is never enough.

'Is it really worth it, Abdul?' I say to him this morning as he hoists me gently into the wheelchair for the day's journey and makes sure that I am strapped in. He keeps silent as he folds up the heavy black sheet that we were lying on at night and puts it into his backpack. 'All this effort, for what? You are so young with your whole life ahead of you, but I have only a few more years ahead of me, at the most.'

The ground begins moving in front of me and I can feel the wheels turning over the grassy path and juddering over the small stones in the ground. Abdul tries so hard to avoid the bumps, but it is impossible on a journey of this length and magnitude. He's an intelligent boy of few words, though when he speaks he makes them count. 'Anaa Basima, please don't say that to me again. I have told you how much you mean to me so many times.' Perhaps I have said it before. He needs to hear it, as much as I need to hear him tell me of my worth. 'Besides, only in the West can we get you the best medical treatment that you need to help you with your spinal trauma, and to keep you away from those beasts that hound you.'

He means the Taliban. Twice in the past few years since Hamed passed away the Taliban took advantage of my old age and relative isolation in our house in Kabul to take my dignity and throw it to the dogs. A shrivelled up woman like me? What were they thinking? They were more ferocious than wild animals, inflamed with hate and power. The first time was bad enough. Abdul's parents insisted that I move in with them for protection but I refused, wanting to hold on to the little I had of Hamed in the house that he had built. The second time, they damaged my spine with their forcefulness and I've not been able to move without assistance since. I was shaking so much with the shock and trauma that Abdul's parents moved me into their house and this time I didn't protest. I lay there flat on a bed for months, dried out and numb like gnarled old pine-tree bark, before Abdul approached me with the idea of escaping to England. He wanted to get medical help for me and to protect me from further harm. Abdul's father has a good teaching job in Kabul so he and the rest of the family did not want to risk the travel to Europe at this time. 'You go with our blessings,' Massoud told me with tears in his eyes. 'Abdul will take care of you and get you the best medical treatment.'

Abdul loves me with a fierce intensity. I know that. But he also harbours ambitions for himself, which is only good and proper. 'There are no opportunities for me here, Anaa Basima. University places are so limited. How many of the 80 students that graduated from Rahman Baba High School last year got a place at university?'

'I don't know, my son. Perhaps 10 or 12?'

'No, Anaa, a mere five! And that is from one of the good schools in Kabul. I am not so ignorant as to assume I could quickly get a place on an engineering course in England, but I'd have more chance there than I would in 10 years here in Afghanistan. At least I have good English skills...'

I keep losing track of where we are on our journey; it seems as though we have been travelling now for months and months. Abdul has to keep telling me where we are. At the moment we're somewhere near the border between the Ukraine and Poland. One part of me wishes that he had just left me behind but a spirit of adventure keeps me going, plus the lack of realistic other options at this point in our journey. We're surviving on three sets of clothes each, and frequently Abdul is getting water from different sources and storing it up in our four litre capacity bottle for daily drinking and clothes washing.

Just yesterday a man wearing military uniform accosted us in an unknown language. I kept my head down and tried to look inconspicuous, but watched carefully everything that was going on. The man held his hand palm up and rubbed his forefingers and thumb together. 'We have no money or travel documents,' Abdul told him in English and held his hands up in the air. This was partially true. We did have a stash of Ukrainian hryvnia and a handful of euros in a hidden place under the wheelchair. The soldier frowned at him uncomprehending. I didn't know what the soldier was going to do to us. Probably he just wanted to intimidate us and see if Abdul would be cowed enough to give him some money, but Abdul is not easily cowed. At that point, two Europeans—a man and a woman—walked past along the railway line that we were travelling and asked us if we needed any help. They spoke in Pashto. Then they began talking in strong voices to the soldier in the unknown language. He argued back for a couple of minutes then seemed to give up and walked away, shrugging his shoulders.

The European man was red-haired and handsome and the woman was tall and pink faced. She kept smiling at us. 'Is this your grandmother?' she asked Abdul.

'Yes,' he said.

'How long have you been travelling?' the man asked.

'About five months so far.'

'And have you been pushing your grandmother the whole way?' the woman said, smiling.

'Yes, of course. There is no other way. We don't trust those people who say that they will take us by boat. We've been covering about 15 km a day, through some difficult terrain but mostly on flat land to save the wheels and protect my grandmother's back from too much jolting.'

'Wow, when pushing a wheelchair that is pretty impressive! Where are you hoping to get to eventually?' she said.

'England... we hope!'

'Please, walk with us a little way,' the man said, putting his hand on Abdul's shoulder. 'Do you have any need for water at the moment?'

'Yes actually, our water is just about to run out,' Abdul said. Incredibly they had a supply of water that they were able to use to fill up our bottle. They were from a charity working with refugees and were patrolling the routes used by many of the refugees and migrants to help with their material needs. They asked us what our story was and Abdul told them an edited version. He left out the fact that I had moved from my own home into his parent's family home. I think he sensed that that would not help our case. I would have done the same. It's better to be cautious rather than too naïve. They warned us that it might be better for us to travel via Poland instead of Hungary, (which had been our original plan) as the Hungarians were currently making the free flow of refugees through their country very difficult. Bridget and Sam, as they were called, walked with us for half an hour or so and we shared stories.

'After all you have been through, you have shown such resilience in going all this way to seek a better life for yourselves. I truly admire you,' Bridget told us.

'What other choice did we have?' Abdul shrugged his shoulders. 'Stay and become more downtrodden or leave and find freedom.'

'See what a good boy he is,' I said, pointing my thumb at Abdul and grinning at Bridget and Sam. They laughed in affirmation.

Today, my spirits have lifted as a result of our encounter with the charity workers. My back is hurting, but it is hurting less than previously as they also provided us with a small supply of ibuprofen tablets. My words to Abdul have been negative, but this is more out of habit than a reflection of how I feel. As I sit in my wheelchair and Abdul pushes, I lift my right arm over my left shoulder and grasp hold of Abdul's hand as it clutches the handlebars. He needs me as much as I need him. I must never forget that.

My thoughts turn to my beloved Hamed. Although my short term memory is erratic, I can remember as clearly as though they were yesterday some of the conversations that took place 30 or 40 years ago.

'When I married you I took you for the adventure of walking with you through life together and so far it's been an eye-opening, heart-warming, joy-giving adventure,' the 'poet' Hamed had said to me one morning, while the open window cast a yellow glow on the polished wooden chair on which he sat.

I moved away from the window at which I was watching the children play and held his face in my hands, 'You say such beautiful, encouraging things, my dear beloved. I'm not perfect but I try to be a good wife.'

'You're the best of wives,' he had said. 'Knowing what you're like gives me confidence that you could face whatever life throws at you, if I pass away before you.'

I had laughed and shoo shooed his comment, but now, as I remember it, I find confidence in the here and now. I swallow back the pool of tears that threatens to rise and I hold my head high. Tomorrow we will cross the border into Poland and be well over two thirds of our way, *inshallah*. The road is long, bumpy and hazardous, but I will greet the future with a lion's pounce and shake of my mane.

Safe from Home by Mark Brayley

The general's daughter sat

at the desk and declared,

"More!"

More of what,

she could not say.

Her mother tongue was torn

apart by her father's trade.

She completed course after

course after course

on the campus

but was never known

for how she related

to the war.

Her homeland shuddered

under her father's hand

but she was sheltered

under the safety of the general's money

and the books they bought,

course after course.

Thus protected,

a tower for refuge,

she never really learnt

but always demanded

more.

The Lake by Catherine Coldstream

The Lake
Took them,
They said.

But my German wasn't good enough to
Understand Them
And They.
Sie und sie.

Der See nahm sie,
Sie sagten.
And I cried
Looking at the still surface
And the sky dark
With half remembered
Faces, and their
Unspoken
Promises.

The Lake
Took them
We repeated, in
Our best German,
When the time came for us,
To go back home.

And we boarded the little
Skiff and put out from the shore,
Knowing
Nothing in
Particular. Only the
Forever unanswered
Silence.

Of
Them and They.
Sie und sie.

Evensong by Louise G. Cole

Head bowed, gaze hung low

she steps the long queue shuffle,

barbs of razor wire boundaries

only a scratch away, a catch caught in transit

before a snatch, a glance upwards,

some heavenly thread pulling taut to loosen

all thoughts of tomorrow, of sorrow,

an opencast mine of majesty

taking her breath away

as the evening presents a Turner sunset

streaking the darkening horizon

into a two dimensional paint chart

of yellow, orange and red,

Syrian Silk, Moroccan Melody,

Cinnabar Sunday, Damascene Dusk,

smudged across the pastel blue emulsion

of a smooth spring sky,

thumb print bruises of purple

cut with slashes of vermillion

backdrop to a slip-sliding streak

of sleek-shine starlings

a union of thousands in fluid acrobatic dance

throwing dark twisted shapes

like newlywed lovers embracing the first dance.

She remembers that day,

recalls the hope,

finds herself smiling.

Running through New York
by Priya Guns

The flame on the stove crackled. The lid of one pot rattled above a sea of bubbling water. Sand and dirt brushed in the wind, and palms gently swayed. The air smelt of the harbour, muddy sands, and oil stained trees. Curry leaves swam in a pot of milk *sothi*. Turmeric stained the mixture muddy. Onions and fenugreek floated atop for air. Senthuran watched as his mother poured some of the boiling water in a tumbler, and then added tea leaves to the pot of what was left. The leaves slowly emitted soft brown hues, none of which he thought were as beautiful as his mother's cinnamon complexion.

The bag of rice flour they had was running short. Weevils weaved through mounds of the fine powder, their antennae detecting pebbles from fine hairs. An assortment of surprises came packed in international aid. The trucks had come in lines and people gathered to receive bags of rations. Senthuran had asked a *Thatha* where the gifts had come from, 'New Yok,' the *Thatha* replied pulling up his *sarem* above his knobbly grey knees.

'Drink,' his mother passed him the tumbler she prepared to one side.

'Senthu, we need fish tonight. This drink will make you brave,' his mother said. Senthuran inhaled the aromatic smell of coriander. Thinly sliced ginger refined the perfect amount of spice and sweet palm sugar melded the *kothumalli thani* smooth. He supped from the hot tumbler slowly.

She poured *sothi* onto some *idiyappam*, the yellow mixture quickly soaked into the stringy webs of rice flour stacked on Senthuran's plate. As he ate, tiny strings from the *idiyappam* stuck onto his skinny fingers like worms, *sothi* dripped from the corner of his mouth. 'Senthuran,' he heard the waters call. The singing fish and mermaids joined in chorus, We're sorry.'

His mother sat cross legged. Her brown feet were ashy from the sand, as if chalk dust was rubbed onto them. The fabric of her sari stretched, creating a hammock of motley colours on her lap. Loose threads frayed along the shawl like hairs blowing in the wind. She looked out vacantly at the water. The waves crashed into memories, reverberating screams in her mind. She rolled a ball of *iddiyappam* until her fingers slowly pruned in the *sothi*, drying stains of turmeric around her nails.

'Amma eat!' Senthuran said. She shook her thoughts and smiled, putting the ball of food into her mouth. She stared at the faint lines on the curry leaf stuck onto her plate, and read them like lines in the palm of her own hand.

'When will we go to New Yok, *Amma?*' he asked. 'New Yok life superr. Like film stars. All people having money, money, *kasa, kasa.* Everything good coming to New Yok,'

Senthuran said in English, showing off proudly to his mother, gesturing for a smile.

'I don't know *rasa*,' she said brushing his cheeks with the back of her hand. He could smell the fenugreek in the sothi from the tips of her tapered fingers.

Senthuran looked down at his gnarled feet. He imagined a pair of crimson football trainers, with crisp white socks over his knees. He'd teach boys to bowl like Muralitharan. They'd cheer his name down the busy streets, 'Sen-thu-ran, Sen-thu-ran.' They'd run for ice cream after matches, him painting the city red in his crimson trainers. The *Thatha* in the *sarem* had said, 'In the Nu Yok number one icekream. Number one peezah. Best beauties. Vite skin and blue colour *kaangal*. Absoluutely Suuperr.'

The words slithering from the *Thatha* astonished Senthuran. He watched as he articulated each word from his tongue, speckled with tiny black burns. Senthuran found the old man's English was eloquent, and the knowledge he shared, inspiring. He never imagined a man from Kallady could walk the streets of New York, staring into eyes as blue as the sea.

'Vi *Thatha* you in Kallady? Vi no New Yok?' Senthuran asked.

'Vife no like Nu Yok,' the *Thatha* replied.

'*Amma*, do you want to move to New Yok?' Senthuran asked his mother.

'Yes *rasa*' she smiled as she sipped on a tumbler of tea. Senthuran was relieved, he wanted those red trainers. He eyed his feet. One blue size 7 Bata slipper on the left, one burgundy size 8 Bata slipper on the right.

His sister loved the colour magenta; burgundy was the closest to magenta they could find. He remembered the day they found the slippers, a memory not easily shaken from his mind. The market was a bustling place, people passing shoulder to shoulder, stripe after stripe of coloured squares from the grid patterned sarems on display, and rainbow coloured saris draped over windows and wrapped endlessly around poles. The colours and textures reflected the mosaic of life passing by.

'*Kothu*, *Kothu*,' men shouted from their roti stands. The sounds of dicing machetes on iron plates, rhythmic and tribal, sacrificing mutton and poultry to a throng of salivating mouths, fish searing, summoning flocks of tongues and palates. Church bells rang and the *adhan* compelled the worshippers to pray, the sounds resonated in orchestrated time.

Bright toy balls from vendors' stalls decked the sides of their stands, and knock-off designer shades, reflected the faces passing by. Sports clothes and sneakers bundled and modelled in sets, Adibas, Nika, and Feebok. Senthuran dreamed of the day he could afford a pair of classic Feeboks, his dark skin in contrast with the white shoes.

'Come boy. Good discounts here today!' a man shouted. Senthuran looked up to see a behemoth. His large arms had straggly black hairs leaping out towards him, pearls of sweat hung on to his dirty brown skin, and his giant paunch pushed towards Senthuran. Senthuran's gaze caught the dark nipples beaming through the Behemoth's *banyan*, like eyes wide and menacing. His sister Kunju held him, 'Let's go,' she said. Senthuran stood still. One straggly hair jutting through the eyes of the *banyan* pointed towards a plastic water rifle. It had a bright orange holster. The package showed a boy with aviator shades, holding the Berf Water

Fire 3.1 series around a group of coveting friends. He slowly walked towards it, pulled by magnetic forces.

'Senthu, come on. Let's go,' Kunju said.

'Let him see sister,' the Behemoth snapped. He moved his large feet closer to Kunju, his eyes examining her tiny frame. He reached out his paw. The silk of her top brought shivers to his spine, the scales on his skin lifted. Senthuran turned over to his sister. The expression he saw on her youthful face was one he hadn't seen before. In an instant he saw her for who she was; vulnerable and exquisite. She was the Goddess Sita bound with glorious light.

He grabbed two plastic bags of Bata slippers and ran to grab Kunju's hands.

'Like magenta,' Senthuran said to his sister, as they sat on the hot sand admiring their new Bata slippers. She smiled forcefully, holding his sweaty hands tight. Her hands were bigger. She smiled at the thought of him grown.

'Senthu!' his mother called, crashing melodic sound, a quake to his thoughts. She handed him a cup of bait, hoping today would be the day he caught his first fish.

He stepped onto the hot sands, watching the fishermen scavenge for parts of their boats, children ran around dilapidated houses, finding fun in the small things. The smell was still pungent.

Dozing in and out of reality, from Batticaloa to New York, he dreamed of the Empire State building, the succulent hotdogs he had never eaten, dripping with fat, the toy stores and water guns, the popping buttery popcorn and the bright night lights. He worshipped the thought of the skyline, back to the sands and lagoons, the sea, and the lands that kept tragedy in the rough. He dreamed of things big and small.

A rattling sound begged his attention. A *kalawathan* was

digging through his cup of bait. He scurried with worms and beetles in his scaly mouth.

'Get back you Godzilla! This is my New Yok!' Senthuran shouted picking up his blue Bata size 7 slipper, he whipped it at the *kalawathan*. The lizard scampered away.

It hopped on the hot land scorched by the sun, quickly manoeuvring around the rubble. Senthuran's calloused feet laboured to keep up, looking towards the *kalawathan* and keeping eyes on the ground to avoid the debris from piercing the hardened soles of his feet. He moved theatrically, mimicking the strides of a large lizard. With each hop he was reminded of the waves, the cries, and the oil in the flood, the people hanging from the palms, and the tears that spate the waters higher.

'Godzilla!' Senthuran screamed.

He ran like Dr. Niko ducking the lizard's atomic breath, fearful for the doom of his people and the destruction of his glorious city. He ran past pretzel stands near Madison Square Garden, past the big N and the welcoming Y. 'Godzilla!' he shouted again.

Surrounded by piles of waste and rubble, Senthuran froze. His chest pounding as sweat trickled down his brow. The *kalawathan* stopped. His beady eyes stared into Senthuran's, and his scaly head twitched. Godzilla ran away.

Senthuran's eyes fixated on where the *kalawathan* had stood. His heart was racing and sinking into the bile in his stomach. His mouth began to dry and his tongue was numb. He moved closer. A burgundy size 8 Bata slipper lay between heaps of rubble. His feet moved slowly, the waves flashing back, he moved rocks and pulled pieces of wreckage from the mound. The cries of thousands echoed in his ears, screaming for help and mercy. He rummaged through the heap, sweat pooling on his face, and there it was. A leg. A dainty leg crushed between horror and fright. It had five beautiful toe nails once painted magenta red, black and dim with death.

The Milk by Naomi Hamill

We found her, just four months ago, the woman who saved our baby. Her face, so wrinkled with lines. Her eyes hidden, as the skin of her eyelids, now so well worn, sagged over her eyes. I recognised her though. How can one forget such a beautiful face and such a beautiful, shining soul? Her eyes said that she recognised me too, although she hasn't many words these days. Her daughter told me that her voice left her the day that liberation came, as if all her words of ecstasy and joy had floated into the sky in a final celebratory poem and silence was all that was needed ever after. As if there was no more she could utter into this dark, joyous, brutal, unfathomable world. She had seen it all, heard it all and now she had spoken it all too. It made me wonder if we only have so many words allotted to each lifetime—the shy, thoughtful types never using their full quota and the talkative types silenced before their time.

Anyway, we found her. I thought that she would still be in that house, but the fear of the memories and the damp, muddy leaves I had to sleep on too many nights kept me from that place. I wanted to knock on the door and tell her that I loved her, above all people I loved her: but the memories of the walk of the weary and the frightened froze my feet; the terrible feeling of cradling a weakening baby froze my arms, and the desperation of trying to squeeze milk from breasts that were undernourished themselves froze my heart.

It was after days and days of uncertain walking; we didn't know what the outcome would be. We didn't know where we were really heading or why we were really walking. We just knew we had to stay hidden. Couldn't be found. Had to keep the children away. Mustn't let them get to us. And why? Because we were who we were. Because of our eagle hearted ancestors and the red flag of our lips and the soft, shy utterances of our mouths. Because we dared to bring more Shqiptar children to life, because we wanted our words to be recognised. Not adored or venerated or made higher than any others. But just to count, just to matter, just to be able to sing our old songs and tell our old stories and to exist. Just to exist.

I was grumpy, I admit it. My arms were weighed down, carrying the child I had borne only two months before. I cursed his birth, although I knew that really I was cursing them, those who had caused this misery. 'Why bring a child into this bitter world?' I said to my husband. 'To be hunted and hated and dispersed and despised. The agony of birth to be confronted so soon with the agony of death?' I had given up. I sat in the mud and I refused to go on. 'Let them catch me,' I said. 'I want a chance to scratch my nails down one of their hard faces,' I said. 'I will dig into their skin so deeply and stare into their eyes and ask them why a child, so small and unknowing, should be subjected to this.'

'You're tired,' my husband said. 'You need a rest. Let me carry the baby. You go on with the others and I'll walk slower behind you all.' I hadn't told him about the milk flow beginning to change.

I had tried to feed the baby that morning and he'd screamed, demanding more, as the white liquid, thin and watery, dribbled from my nipple. He'd sucked and sucked but the flow was so weak, a pathetic attempt at nourishment, and he'd created a scene. I couldn't blame him. But bread and biscuits and the jarred peppers hadn't lasted very long and although the others gave me what they could from their rations, my body was beginning to rebel.

'He's hungry,' I said. 'The milk isn't coming so much. I'm not eating enough and I can't keep feeding him on nothing. I'm worried that soon it will dry up and he'll die, just like his brother did before him.'

My husband is a serious man. He did not try to make me feel better or say that this was not the case. But he called the other children and his brother and his wife and his uncle and his aunt and he explained the situation to them all. 'We must give,' he told our own small ones quietly. 'For the baby, we must give. And you will be hungry tonight. And you may be hungry tomorrow. But we will find help and we will not be hungry forever. Give your food to your mother.' They did so, little angels, and although their faces told me differently, they were happy to keep their tiniest brother alive. And although each mouthful tasted of guilt, I knew that this must happen.

Sleeping under the trees, covered in plastic sheets that would frost each morning, I wondered if we would have to sacrifice this little one for them all. *You're going crazy,* my mind told me. But these situations and this terror and the walking, the walking, the walking, made me think in these unnatural terms. I almost laughed when I thought of the hundreds of German marks we had, ready to bribe the soldiers, but nowhere to spend it and no food to buy. What a ridiculous situation we found ourselves in.

Before I awoke, my husband and his brother had searched the area. A house, not far away. But were they friends or enemies? Did they want us alive or dead? And would their cow, standing promisingly in the garden, have milk for a family and for a little soul not yet comfortable enough in the world to know if it would stay?

'I think that I should go,' I said. 'They will listen to a woman. Even if they are enemies, surely the hardest heart cannot ignore a mother's pleas to keep her child alive?' I knew that this was not the case, but I didn't want my husband or his brother to be seen, knowing that they were particularly after the men.

As I knocked on the door, I felt such relief. I could hear the sweet sounds of Albanian being spoken and then this face, the one now so worn and so silent, was there and she was saying that yes they did have a cow and that yes, it produced good milk and then no, no they would not sell it to me.

They wouldn't sell the milk to me.

They wouldn't sell the milk.

My baby cawed a little in my arms.

'I will give you milk. There will be no charge. And what else do you need? You must come in and rest.'

We didn't know this woman but we huddled into her sitting room and she gave us bread and tea and milk and peppers. She gave us warmth and comfort and peace and hope. If only for a short time.

'Why are you not heading on further?' my husband asked. 'They may come here. They may find you.'

'We are too old for running,' said her husband. 'If they

come, they come. God will decide. We have sent away our families and we pray each day for their safe return.'

We stayed there for three nights. It was hard to leave. Milk each day, the warmth of walls, a cow to cheer up the little ones, bread, tea, kindness. It was hard to leave.

Not too long after that, the liberators came. We'd made it to a higher village and we stayed in the barns and houses as trucks rolled into town. Arrivals from yesterday told us that the liberators were coming. But, of course, we couldn't trust. All the years of trust that life had taught us had been undone in just a few short weeks.

But the UN sign on the side of the vehicles told us this was true. And we went into the streets, every one of us. Probably three thousand people in that tiny village; we all went outside and the children had no idea what was going on. But they could see that we were happy, for the first time in months. 'Are we going to stop walking now mama?' one of my smallest asked me.

'Yes,' I replied. 'No more walking.'

'Ne jemi te lire,' we shouted. We shook hands with men who didn't speak our language. We touched our hearts. We shed tears, of course. We sang our songs. The children gazed adoringly at the khaki trucks and these people who had come from places they'd never seen, to save us.

I held our baby aloft and I said a silent prayer; I thanked that man and that woman aloud, even if I was only talking to the sky. I asked God to bless them and I blessed them myself and thanked them again and again and again.

I held our baby aloft. High. In the air. My precious trophy of survival.

Milanese Feast by Emma Kittle-Pey

As the murmur of voices buzzed around my head I began to hear just hear one soloist, coming from behind where I sat at the breakfast table.

'We're in Milan. People go shopping in Milan. It's like Manhattan. If we're not going shopping then I might as well go. Are you going to give me some money? Are you *not* going to give me some money?'

I looked into rather than through the glass of the window. I could see a teenager with her parents. Staring at her phone. A prima donna. I went back to my pile of carbs from the all-you-can-eat buffet. I got everything, there was still an abundance of food even when I arrived. I'd been expecting it ravaged and savaged, but no; an overflowing tray of croissants, and pastries, a bucket of cake, biscuits in a bottomless pot. Fruit, half peaches, yoghurt, cereals. Ham, cheese, apricots. I tried not to overdo it, but it was hard.

'It's Milan. You've got to give me money. Oh god. You're not going to. That really sucks.'

I ate my croissants, and drank my juice. I stared out of the window. It wasn't what I'd expected from Milan, the view of a concrete terrace I'd have found at home. But it didn't matter. To be alone, for no one to know, to stop that constant two lives, the one inside and the one for show. To stop everything.

The men beside me chatted, I could see the intensity in the face of the guy from earlier. He'd pranced to one of the spare tables and put his bag on a seat, claiming it as his own, moaning and whining to his partner about the queue. But their voices were dull in comparison to the girl behind me. The ache above my eyes was prodded by her notes, her tune in crescendo.

'You want me to take my tray over there?'

'I want you to take your tray over there.' Her dad a resolute double base to her vivace violin.

'I'm not taking my tray over there. It's full up.'

'I want you to take your tray over there. Because that's what people do.'

Her voice swayed above the swarm of voices, soaring over it now like an angry clarinet. But the buzz settled, reduced, quietened for her performance. The men next to me, and other heads, started to look around a little too.

'I'm not taking the tray. I can see some other people not taking their trays.'

'I want you to give me your cell-phone and take the tray.'

I turned again, properly, toward this voice.

I saw the girl looking at the tray area and back again and to it again. 'Are you trying to humiliate me?' She says.

'No. Give me your cell phone and take the tray.'

It was that tiny uncomfortable fidgeting look she gave the tray trolley. And then the second one. And the third.

The ache left my head, fell into the back of my throat and sank into my stomach. I remembered a hundred moments of our youth in that second and I nearly wept for her and him, and the mum that had already left them to it.

I got up with my tray and as I passed I stopped at their table. 'I'm taking my tray. Do you want to come with me?'

The girl stared at my navel, then the dad looked up and said, 'We don't speak.'

But I did it again. I thrust my idea forward, I risked everything, and I said, 'But do you want to just come with me? I'm taking my tray.'

The girl rose, head bent, with her tray, and the dad said, 'Oh. Thank you.' She followed me to the tray trolley. There's no room. We lifted them onto the top, the orange glass sliding to one side above my head, but I somehow managed to balance it before it fell. First my tray, then hers.

The Photo by Aoife Lyall

Face down, he could have tripped

in his eagerness to reach the waves:

to feel the delicious biting

froth foam on his bare legs; to gasp

as his favourite denim shorts slowly drown

in salted spray to quench their sudden thirst.

Or maybe he simply fell asleep on the warm dry sand,

enchanted by the gentle heat and giving pressure;

wrapped in a dream as the sea curls in around him,

his favourite red t-shirt bunched with gentle turns,

raised over the jutting hip of a growth spurt,

his faced turned, coy, as though in sleep

he sees the photos saved for future birthdays.

Just out of sight, perhaps, a mother

ready to scoop him up in tender arms

as the sea soaks through the soles

of cartooned shoes and cartooned

socks, knowing she will wipe the wet sand

from his laughing crying lips, sing sweet

low notes to soften the crash of small

swells that threaten him, and wrap

him in a sun-drenched towel to draw

the sea from his soft skin.

Only, no.

His arms are by his side.

His upturned hand, too white for sleep.

The man who scoops him up, a stranger.

(For Alan Kurdi)

Leavings by Petra McQueen

Ania tries to ignore the postcard propped against the bedside lamp. She has never stolen anything before: not a penny from a pile of loose change, a bar of soap, or even a discarded pen. Nothing, in all these years of cleaning. But there's something about the postcard. She imagines slipping it into her apron pocket, feeling its shape and weight as she wipes and polishes. Dragging her attention away, she scans under the bed to check for the usual leavings: discarded knickers, odd socks, and ear buds. There's only fluff. Using her foot, she clicks on Henry-the-Hoover. He whooshes into life, face beaming and shiny. Of all the chambermaids at the Windermere, she's the only one who looks after the equipment. And she's the most efficient. Eight minutes thirty-three seconds per room. Wonder-Woman. Huk. Huk. In. Out. Kaboom.

But, today, as she thrusts Henry back and forth, the postcard slows her, charms her, drags at her. It is the sun and she is a small, cold orbiting planet. She's pulled closer.

The picture is of a church. The tessellated rose and amber bricks remind her of Pisonika's chapel. Could it actually be Saint Adlebert's? She unplugs Henry and picks up the card. In small script on the bottom right hand corner is the legend, 'Greetings from Albany.' She turns over the card. 'Hi Mum, Glad to hear you're better, love Tom.' She translates as best she can. 'Cześć Mamo! Cieszę się, że już lepiej się czujesz. Kocham Cię. Tom.' Now there is a boy who loves his mum. Good. She thinks of Aleksy, four hundred kilometres away, bent double on the flat Fenland plains, hacking fat heads off cabbage stalks. Her arms feel heavy from the lack of embrace.

She sees herself and her strong handsome son, arm in arm, strolling through the streets of Ely. They'd planned for her to travel to his in a month but why wait? She'd ask for Saturday off. They couldn't deny her: she'd worked solidly for five months: filled in for flighty girls with hangovers and pregnancy scares.

A trolley rattles down the corridor. The new girl must be sloppy if she can finish so fast. Ania rests the postcard on the lamp, looks at it for a long moment, then bustles into the en-suite. Seeing that the shower has sprung a leak, she rings reception to alert maintenance. She completes six more rooms in fifty-three minutes. Equipment swiftly put away, she trots to the staff quarters to be first on the phone but the new girl is already there.

Waiting, hands in pocket, Ania thinks how happy Aleksy will be when he hears she's coming sooner than planned. They'll visit the Cathedral café and drink macchiato. Because Aleksy has the internet, he'll have all the gossip on Pisonika. She'll find out if Elzbieta married that dope-head; if the Wartość Shop is still flogging day-glo toilet roll; and how Zuzanna's chemo is going. Ania itches to know. Here she learns nothing. She can't get a phone signal and has to pay a fortune to use the wifi.

The new girl guffaws, sings out something like 'santeesana' and clatters the phone into the cradle. Her wide smile drops as she turns. Ania rushes past, keys in her personal charge-number, and dials. It rings and rings. Perhaps Aleksy can't hear it above the bone-rattling tractor. She tries again. It rings twice and clicks off.

She goes to the room which is no longer hers alone. The new girl is there. She's sprawled on her bed, dressed only in bra and pants, brilliant white against her black skin. Her uniform is discarded on the floor.

'I am sorry for bad mess.' Tears varnish her cheeks.

Ania backs out. There are four hours to kill until evening dish-washing. She meanders into the staff lounge where the television soundlessly shows a couple being shown around an empty house. Hunched in a cluster of chairs, three bellboys are having a desultory game of poker. On the other side of the room, Khrystyna, one of the receptionists, is reclining on a beat-up sofa, painting her nails mauve. Tinny pop pulses from her headphones. Ania chooses an armchair next to the empty Coke machine. She flicks through 'Cumbrian Life' and gazes out of the window. Horizontal splashes of rain mark the glass. She stands. At the foot of a scarred grey hill, a lone sheep grazes.

The door bangs open. It is the supervisor. Everyone stops what they are doing, and watches as he strides up to Ania. 'Go to Room 402. Plumber's left crap everywhere.' Seeing she hasn't followed every word, he barks, 'Clean!' and waves his fist as though holding a cloth. 'Room-'

'402,' says Ania in English. 'I know.'

She clatters down the service stairs, picks up her cleaning

stuff and hurries along the corridor and into Room 402. The postcard is exactly where she left it. After sprucing up the bathroom, she slips the card into her apron pocket and, heart beating, scurries back to her room. The new girl is asleep. Ania perches on her own bed and takes the postcard out of her pocket. She traces the edges; they're rough as though handled many times before.

The new girl opens her eyes. They are shot with red.

'What's that?'

Ania doesn't answer, puts the postcard back in her pocket and leaves. Seeing a long queue at the telephone, she fetches her coat and exits via the kitchens. Pulling up her collar, she traipses past the gatehouse. Dry stone walls offer no shelter. What a place! She'd thought herself lucky to have landed this job. She would've been better picking cabbages with Aleksy.

She negotiates a stile and trudges up a tussocky field. Half way to the summit, she fishes out her phone. Tiny spots of rain glisten on the screen. In the top right hand corner, a line flickers on and off. She walks. One bar. Two! That should do it.

It's so windy she fears Aleksy won't be able to hear her. He doesn't pick up anyway. She tries again. Nothing. Should she stay out longer? A squall bounces up the valley, flurries the grass, whips her skirt. Above, a dingy cloud brews. Even the dullest day was never as miserable as this in Pisonika.

About to clamber back over the stile, she spots her roommate tramping along the road lugging a tattered holdall. Ania ducks behind the stone wall and waits until the girl is out of sight. She returns to the hotel. On her roommate's bedside table, stands a framed photograph. It shows a little girl. She has a t-shirt with a diamante heart embossed on it. Ania puts down the photograph and takes out the postcard.

She looks at it for a long time. The wind picks up and rattles the sash windows. She slips the postcard under her pillow and settles down.

A rap wakes her. The supervisor is at the door. Next to him is Khrystyna.

'This dick,' said Khrystyna in Polish, nodding at the supervisor, 'wants to know if you've seen a postcard from Room 402. A postcard! Who the hell cares about a postcard?'

'I haven't seen it.' Her heart thumps.

Looking at the supervisor, Khrystyna lifts her eyebrows. 'She hasn't seen it. I told you.'

He turns on his heel. Khrystyna rolls her eyes and follows. Alone, Ania feels the postcard burning beneath the pillow. She takes it out, hand ready to screw it up. But she can't. The church is so homely, so innocent. She thinks of Aleksy at his confirmation, face scrubbed and shining.

Ania puts the postcard in her pocket and hurries to the phone. She's lucky. No one's there. She wills Aleksy to pick up the phone, to hear the deep delighted 'Cześć Mamo!'

Two rings.

'Hello?' An English girl.

Flustered, Ania struggles to form a sentence. 'This who?'

She hears Aleksy laugh.

'Mamo?'

'Who was that?'

'What?'

'Don't give me that. Who was on the phone?'

'Only Nicki. She's staying with me for a bit. Got chucked out—'

Ania replaces the phone. In her bedroom, she slumps onto the bed. How could she stay with Aleksy now? A girl changed everything. Last time the boys had bunked together so she could sleep alone in Aleksy's room; she was damned if she was going to share with an English floozy. But what was worse than all of that, was the joy in his voice. As though he hadn't been ignoring her calls for two weeks.

Her roommate comes in with her infernal smile, dragging the holdall at her heels. 'Hello,' she says.

Ania wants to leave but there's nowhere to go.

Tilting the bag, the woman pours the contents onto the bed. Out spills ropes of necklaces, shiny plastic bangles, dazzling wraps, and savanna animals made of beads and wire.

Ania stares.

'You like?' the woman asks.

She shakes her head.

The woman looks glumly at the objects. 'Shop no like either.'

Ania isn't surprised. The stuff is too bright for these dull hills.

'I need school money for my little girl.' The woman cradles her arms, gently raising one elbow up and down. She mimes the action so well that Ania conjures Aleksy as a baby. What a solid, plump weight he'd been. But only when asleep. Awake, he'd arched his back as though striving to escape. As soon as he could, he'd toddled into the yard and peered through the slats in the fence. He was always looking outwards, outwards. Every day for a decade, she had to bang a wooden spoon on a pan to call him back from play. 'Aleksy! Alekseeeee!' Eventually, he'd emerged slimed with mud, sticky buds clinging to his shirt.

'You can't come when I call?'

'Sorry.'

She would always forgive him. He had thick black lashes

that butterflied against his cheeks. So handsome. Shopkeepers were always pressing lollies and buns on him.

A gust of air brings Ania back to the present. The woman is flapping out a sarong, pulling the bright cotton tight, folding it, smoothing down edges. Ania thinks how it came all the way from Africa, smelling of cloves, packed in a suitcase. Ania brought nothing except what she could carry on the plane.

'How did you get a visa?' Ania asks.

'I myself am citizen of Europe.' There is silence as the woman tucks and folds another sarong. She sighs, capitulating to Ania's unspoken questions, 'My husband was German. He live with me in Kenya. He die. The money finish. Here I am.'

'I'm sorry.'

The woman continues to shake and fold the fabric. There is such concentrated sorrow in the simple action that Ania feels a tug in her own heart.

Khrystyna pops her head around the door. 'I heard you're selling earrings?'

The woman beams and pats the bed. Khrystyna sits down and they trawl through a pile of plastic. Ania leaves. The corridor is empty. Taking out the postcard, she looks at it, thinking of Aleksy's father for the first time in years. They were married in St. Adlebert's and though not a single candle guttered, her bridegroom died before the year was out. A month later Aleksy was born, thrusting back her grief in a rush of sleepless nights, anxiety and nappies. She was too busy, too busy to grieve even when her parents died one after another three years later and were buried in the grounds of St. Adlebert's.

She kept going, content as long as Aleksy was safe. They

could've lived for ever in Pisonika, but Aleksy wanted more. He paced the small living room, 'Oh, Mum, let's go. Just for a year or so. Save up. Buy a shop. Give the Wartość a run for their money.'

His dream, never hers. She did what he wanted because she never wanted him to leave.

She takes a final look at the postcard and makes a decision.

Arriving at Room 402, she kneels down, and starts to slide the postcard under the door.

The door opens 'Can I help?'

Ania stands with the postcard in her hand.

'You found it! Where was it?' The woman has thick curly white hair like a sheep.

'My English no good.'

The woman takes the postcard and clasps it to her chest. 'It's from my son.' Gently, she shuts the door.

Only then does Ania say, in English, 'I too have son. A man.'

And all the way back to her room, she thinks of Aleksy, of how they'll sit in the Cathedral café, and over a macchiato, she'll tell him her plans: how she's going to save up enough money for a little flat in Pisonika, one of the ones off Nowy Swiat, and how, when he's ready he can bring that girl over. Ania will serve periogi, and maybe a little vodka. They'll take a walk into town and she'll show her the sights: the great oaks in Wictoria Park, the spanking shops of the Ojczyzn District and the little chapel of St. Aldebert's where all her memories lie.

The Decision by Suzy Norman

I watch as the eye in a whirlwind, my senses pitchforked;

I see her eyes narrow, his mouth open, close, open-close.

The room turns to liquid.

From the corner of the room, I hear the words he doesn't have the requisite papers.

Arrangements must be made.

This is what they say and I try to listen.

Her coffee cup rests on the edge of the table.

A single bulb hisses above their heads.

I see it all: Their rings; their watches; the expensive cut of her suit;

a dab of toothpaste on his collar; a grey hair swimming against the tide of her centre parting.

Waiting in the corner, I listen to their voices:

a plucked string echoing out; a hum remaining.

Printing by Suzy Norman

Meanwhile, we all wake to snow,

space-edifying and silent at the camp as far as the eye can cope.

From the window, we watch the latticed roof of the garden seat;

an ice waffle.

I head out alone and spy the cat prints.

Next to them, the minute criss-cross of birds—adjacent, a mouse?

Alongside, a noxious badger, or a harmless fox.

I look down to see my feet tarnish the perfect canvas.

I wonder what is this place.

It's no place like home, like no place I've ever known.

Insignificant community; plant-starved landscape;

the distant echo of laughter.

The warning bells ring behind me;

I turn around and head back; silent footfalls,

reversing the prints the animals made.

These marks remind we come and we must return.

The Boy on the Beach by Susan Pope

He pushed his tiny toes into the burning sand and wriggled his little fat feet down to where it was cool and damp. At the water's edge, he could see his father had just pulled his fishing boat onto the shore. The boy laughed and waited for the signal. When the big man had secured the boat he looked up and waved. Little Adou toddled over the hot sand shrieking with laughter. His father lifted him up, swinging him onto his shoulders. The boy screamed bubbling with joy. The man jogged up the beach with the boy held high. It was the best donkey ride in the world and his happiest memory.

Now I'm in the worst place in the world; squashed like a bad melon, faint with hunger, so thirsty my tongue is stuck to the roof of my mouth. I can't move and know I mustn't move. I can hardly breathe as if I lay dying. But I know if I do exactly as I've been told, I'll get back to that happy place with my father. I try not to think about how much I ache and concentrate on more memories; like a video clip I saw once on a phone.

He waved goodbye as his father set off on the boat again. By the shore, he waited for days, but his father didn't return. Adou remembered the soldiers coming to their shack. Father wasn't there, so they took his mother away. After that he was looked after by another woman. She said to call her Auntie. She had six children of her own, so Adou was a nuisance. Food was rationed, and being the smallest he got very little. He wandered along the beach looking for crabs and shellfish. The soldiers told the children to stay off the beach. They put up barbed-wire and signs. He didn't know what the signs meant until the day one of the boys had his legs blown off. After that, he didn't go to the beach.

Worse than being cramped up is the darkness, and not knowing what is happening. Sometimes I am moved and bumped along. Sometimes everything is still. I can hear voices but not what they say. I can smell the sea, and feel the rise and fall of the water. I am a piece of luggage folded and creased. The memories return.

Adou had grown taller and skinnier. Every time he asked Auntie about his mother or his father she made him stand on a stool until he was so dizzy he fell off. If he cried, he was sent outside. 'Snivel in the gutter, gutter child,' said Auntie. He would put his head between his knees, stifling his tears and recall his first happy memory.

One day Auntie said to him. 'Adou, your father is alive and living in Spain.' He didn't know where that was, but Auntie said, 'That's in Europe. That's where we'd all like to go and leave this Ivory Coast behind us.'

Adou said, 'Can I go there and live with my father?' She laughed at him, but later she said she would find out. He thought that was the kindest thing she'd ever said to him.

Weeks passed, then one day Auntie said, 'Your father wants you to go to him. But you will have to be smuggled in. Once you are there they won't send you back if you tell them your father lives in Spain.' He was eight years old now. He hadn't seen his father since he was five, but he felt as if he had been dead all that time and now he was alive again; alive and with hope. He also found it hard to believe his cruel Auntie was suddenly being so good to him.

'Thank you, thank you, Auntie,' he said. 'What do I have to do? When can I go?'

'Once you are there,' said Auntie, 'we can apply to join you because we are your family.' He knew this wasn't so, but didn't argue. He swallowed the tablets she gave him and slept for a long time.

I am awake now and moving once more. As I lie in my cramped dark prison, the person moving me struggles with the weight. I am scared the hiding place will burst open under the strain of my weight and moving on the spindly wheels. There is a lot of shouting and I recognise the voice of the girl who has pushed and pulled me on and off the boat. We must be nearly there, very close to the end of the journey.

I hear a dog barking, and my heart is drumming in my ears. Will I ever arrive to see my father? Will I ever learn the secrets of his wonderful life? 'Please let it happen,' I say in my head. 'Please let it happen.'

The dog is still barking and snuffling around; so close I can smell it. My prison is lifted up and then thumped down again; I feel the shock waves. The girl screams and shouts and men are shouting back. She begins to cry. So do I, while the dog still barks.

Hands fumble with the locks on my suitcase prison, forcing them open. My tiny world is suddenly flooded with light so I close my eyes tight. The stale air I have breathed for days evaporates and my lungs fill with sea air.

Have I arrived at last? Is this Spain? Has my father come to meet me? I open my eyes and see only men in uniform, like the soldiers back home.

Brilliant Disguise by Robert Ronsson

Did you hear the rumour 'bout the guy who was on the roof of the World Trade Center on 9/11 and surfed the building as it went down? Well, it *did* happen. I was that guy. *I* was the Twin Towers Surfer. My name is Jorge Morales. You don't know me, cos I don't exist.

It's still dark when I leave my room but I can tell it's gonna be a fine day. The air is cold but at the end of summer this means sunshine. By the time I come out of the subway it's warming up good. You climb out of the tunnels down there by the Battery and you always look up to check out the towers. It's a squinting day. Those buildings cut into the sky like knife blades.

From where I live, out beyond Harlem, it's only twelve stops on the A-line to Chambers Street and the WTC Plaza. But it's a million miles to me. Up there I walk round easy. Nobody bothers. We know which corners the blue-and-whites favour. I stay away from the joints the NYPD shake down once a week so they can tick their boxes. I sit on the front stoop taking a smoke and can wave 'Hi' no problem.

Down here I keep a watch. One wrong move and I'd be on the bus to Acapulco. Yeah, it's kinda weird for a man of colour to be worried about deportation to Mexico. That's what comes of being born down there to a Mexican mother and African-American father. That sonofabitch dived back across the border as soon as she let slip I was on the way. He may have been a US citizen but it don't make *me* legal. So down here among the suits you learn to walk with your chin low in your collar so you're invisible. Just a glance in the wrong dude's direction and next thing they shouting you stole some lady's purse a block away. If the last thing you want is to be hauled off to the precinct, you brush along the walls like a cat with no home.

I show my security card at the gate. I study the floor. The security guys know. I know they know. It's cos my card don't have no picture. It's not even my name—this guy's first name is Alphonso. I'm a visitor who comes in every day. Everybody who sees that card knows. I'm a wrong'un. One false move and I'm out.

'Yo, Fonzy! Going to be busy today. We got the Port Authority high-roller meeting on 106. That's 25 covers, and some goddam broker has booked out five tables on 107. Get your sorry butt over to those taters.'

It's how I start every day, feed potatoes into a peeling machine, check 'em for bads, put 'em through the hash browns machine. Potatoes in one end, made up hash browns out at the other—hundreds of 'em.

'Let me know when there's enough, Carl,' I shout.

'There's never gonna be enough of them mothers, Fonzy,

not today.' Carl laughs as he pimp-rolls his way to the egg mixer. Carl likes it busy.

Windows on the World is mostly for tourists at night but every day we open for breakfasts from 6.ooam. It's for the suits—their power breakfasts—making deals before the day's started. Us guys, the Alphonsos, the Carls, the people of colour—we're out back, in our green fatigues, oiling the wheels of commerce with hash browns and powdered egg.

I'm on washing-up when the building shakes. It's a good shift. It means I get to scrape the plates—the odd bits of bacon, pancake, hash brown—they all end up inside of me instead of the trash. On a good day I can get through on breakfast alone.

Anyways, I'm by the machine with a mouthful of sausage, scraping and rinsing plates before loading 'em, when the floor moves and there's a rumble below. It's like the building has bad guts or something. I don't see a plane. I don't know what it is. We don't have windows in the kitchens. The suits could've seen it zooming straight at 'em but I had my hands in the trash picking out my breakfast.

'Whoa, Carl! What the...' The floor is shuddering. 'Earthquake!' It feels like the whole building has jumped in the air and is still wobbling like jello.

'Stay cool, Fonzy. You deal with your own shit, man. Leave the worrying to the suits.' He goes off to see what's happening.

The panic gets me as soon as the fire alarms go off and it's difficult to remember how it all pans out. We try the four fire-exit staircases but there's smoke and heat coming up at us in every one like we're heading down into hell. We go back up to the kitchens. There's something like fifty of us kitchen guys running from base to base like Yankees on speed. We gotta find a way out. There's no plan; nobody's being boss. It's each one for hisself.

I decide to go back to the staircase with the least smoke and head up. I don't tell anyone. I think, man, when those helicopters come, I want to be first off.

Well, they don't come. There's no sign of helicopters up in that wide blue sky and I can guess why. There's too much heat coming off that roof and the smoke. On three sides you can tell the fires are getting nearer because of the heat. The pitch under our feet is soft—smoking. So there's around thirty of us in one corner, waiting. The others is all suits.

We can't get near the edge to see what's happening. They all have their cell phones out frantically pressing buttons—but the networks are jammed. Some guy says he saw a plane flying toward the tower. He says it hit about twenty floors below. I think of some suit flying a twin-engine jet and he's late for a meeting. I curse him. None of us knows about terrorists. All them people dying and not knowing why.

There's so much smoke now you can't see nothing. We all search the sky for helicopters that ain't going to come and feel the heat broiling us through that roof. That's when I spy the venting stack. It's right in our corner of the building and about fifteen-feet tall. There's no way of climbing it I can see but I figure maybe there's something on the other side. That's when being invisible acts for me. I slink round and sure 'nough there's a ladder that takes you to the top. Yards above that griddle-plate of a roof has to be a better place to be. So I climb it.

When I get up top it's flat concrete with a short chimney stack in one corner. The whole thing only about four-feet square. The incredible thing is the chimney is putting out cooler, fresh air. I figure it must be coming from below the fire. It's warm but fresher than anything up here. I lie down, curl up so that nothing shows over the edge, put my nose to the opening and wait for help.

Over the side back down on the roof the guys are coughing. They have their shirts up round their faces. The women are taking off their jackets and tearing them into strips to wind round their feet. Everybody's faces are black with smoke. They're frying. I can see by the way their chests are moving that the air is being used up in the fire. They haven't got long. I keep myself real low against that concrete and wonder what happened to Carl.

I only see one jumper—well it was two but they did it together—a man and a woman, both suits. They're having this talk. You can see a big decision is being made. She takes off her shoes. Man, her feet must be on fire. They hold hands and run for the edge together and leap out and over, still holding hands. And she has her shoes in her other hand like she's going to need them when she hits the ground.

An hour goes by so slow watching the guys on the roof go down one by one as the smoke and heat gets them. There's none left standing when the really big tremors start. It's like the floor moves in the funhouse on Coney Island. Cracks start like in earthquake movies. I see bodies slip into a hole as it opens up under them. They go down into the fire.

Then with a huge roar we're all going down, so fast. The sides of the building come out above us and then crash on top. My vent holds together going down in one piece. I'm lying tight down on top of the concrete roof holding on to the chimney like it's the only thing can keep me alive. I cling on as we hurtle down. The noise is like ten subway trains over my head.

Me and this little cement roof we go down and down buffeted and crashed. Man we're like a running-back. No matter what blocks and tackles come our way we jump, swerve and spin but we just keep going. Nothing's going to stop us hitting that touchdown line. And the miracle is the mother always stays flat. We go down while the world disintegrates into a blizzard of building bits that tear at my clothes and skin. We go down and down until it's just me and my island of cement spinning and bucking like a pebble skimming the sea.

And by the time it goes quiet the little roof and me are spewed away from the Plaza. We come to rest across by the Chambers Street subway exit. The little cement roof and me—Super-surfer.

It's all a fog of dust. It settles round me plip-plopping like tropical rain on a tin roof. Some big stuff comes down but misses. Dust clogs everything. I try to strain the air though my nose but it feels like I'm breathing solid lumps. I pick plugs of dust out of my nostrils. I hold my breath and get my face as close to the floor as possible. I put my head over the edge of the roof and find some dustless air beneath it. I breathe again.

Maybe I'm dead. All that noise and movement was crossing to the other side. But I sit up and feel my legs and my arms. They're still there, solid and alive. I pick at the flaps on my fatigues and I try to wipe off the thick crust of white dust. It's set on me like it's glued. I get up and look around. The street is empty. Those that could get away when the building came down have long gone. The others are underneath it.

I start walking, stumbling more like. I can see the top of the Empire State through the fog and I head toward it. I shuffle along like an old man.

The air gets clearer. I'm passed by firefighters running the other way. They're going back. Me? I ain't never going back. I turn into Broadway and start walking north.

For the first time in hours I see civilians—ordinary folks, wandering blank-eyed. And already I feel it and my shoulders stiff up straighter. Like I'm the only one been in a war zone where adrenalin and fear play games with your mind, with your voice, with your bladder. They just don't know. Won't never know like I do.

'Are you all right?' It's a pretty white woman—a suit. She has a frown like she's worried. I turn round but she's talking to me. 'You need to get cleaned up. Were you close when it came down?'

I hear her voice like it's through a cell phone with a bad signal. The roar of me falling through a hundred floors is still gumming up my ears.

She could be the one sends me back so I keep my eyes down. 'Yeah. Lucky I guess.' I try to smile and feel the crust crack on my face.

She touches me gently. Her hand is on my arm. She touches me. 'Let's see if we can find someone for you.'

The roar in my ears is louder. But then I see that she hears it too. She looks up, her eyes wide like she seen a zombie coming for her. 'Not again,' she mouths and starts running back where she came from. I drag my feet behind her. I got no idea why I'm running.

The policeman is standing by his motorcycle—a Harley-Davidson—all shiny blue and white. He steps across to where I'm standing bent over breathing hard after the run. I try to think what he can get me for. I start to shake.

'Hey, mister,' he says. He doesn't stand like they usually do—all cocky, chest out, shiny boots spread apart, daring me to try something. He's bending too as if he's interested. I touch a white, dust-covered finger to my heaving chest.

'Yeah,' he says. 'Are you okay?'

I nod.

'You look as if you've been right there, buddy. Where you heading?'

'Uptown.' I point north.

'How far? I can get you a ride. Where to? Looks like you need the ER yourself. Which hospital?'

'No, no. I'm okay. I feel like I gotta walk.' I shake my head. The last thing I need is to see the inside of a blue and white.

'You sure? You look in bad shape. You should get checked out.'

'No... I'll just...' I point up Broadway again and head uptown.

'You'll know what's best, I guess.' I hear his voice trailing behind. He's talking to some guy else. 'Geez, looka him. He musta been right there.' He's probally got his cap in his hand scratching his head like in a cartoon.

I walk on up Broadway until I'm by the Grand Hotel—the one in SoHo. All the way, people stop when they see me. Some step forward then think better of it. They look at me and then back at the gap in the sky where the towers used to be. They don't know what to do. They look scared.

A black guy, build of a heavyweight boxer, dressed in black, stands in front of the blacked-out windows of the hotel. I nod to him as I pass.

He salutes, putting a finger to the rim of his shades. His head is shaved and shines in the sun. 'Are you all right, sir?' he asks. The 'sir' sounds funny, like he means it.

'Just heading home,' I say.

'How far you got to go?'

'Uptown.'

'You sure you can make it?'

'Sure.'

'We can get you cleaned up in here.' He nods to the door behind him. I glance through and see the cool marble floor and the polished wood. I think I musta heard him wrong.

'What?'

'You can clean up. It's the least we do. We don't have any rooms now—not with what's happened. But you can get rid of the dust.'

I look down at my tunic. The green is showing through where the cake of dust has cracked and fallen away. 'Are you kiddin me?' I say

'You look done in, sir. How long were you there for?'

'From the start. Right from the start.'

He takes off his shades, holds out a huge hand and steps toward me. I step back and freeze. 'Can I shake your hand, sir?' he says.

We shake hands—I'm looking at the shine off his shoes. I tell him, 'I won't come in. Gotta carry on home.'

'Whatever you say, sir.' He does the salute thing again.

As I turn away I see myself in the hotel window. It isn't me, Jorge Morales, looking back. Not even Alphonso. This dude I'm looking at is white, coated in baked-on dust. He touches his white fingers to his white face. His dark eyes are bloodshot from the dust. The green of his paramedic's uniform shows through where the material has creased. This guy has been down at Ground Zero saving lives. He must have got out seconds before the tower came down.

Seeing him makes me think. This is what it's like when you're *somebody*.

Limbo by Nesreen Salem

They had arrived a while ago. Exactly when was a mystery, for time stood still in this new land. Like time, the land stretched in front of them; a marble carpet of yellow; inhospitable and spiteful. But they were told it was only a temporary transit point; a place where they would be sorted and eventually given a new life. A place called Transit.

Transit lay in between Point A and Point B. Point A was where they had migrated from. Saleh could not remember what happened in Point A anymore. No one around him could. Vague residues of pain that this new place outdid in frustration. How long had they been in this place of infinite space and time? How did they arrive and when would they be allowed to leave?

New arrivals appeared every day. They, too, had arrived with the terror they'd seen inscribed on their skins but with the inability to articulate what had happened. Their clothes were soaked but they were not shivering. The Transit was too lifeless for a breeze. No one felt cold or warm. They could feel nothing. Remembered nothing.

Saleh woke up restless. He still couldn't remember how

long they had been in Transit for, but the heavy ball of ageing dragged his soul lower day by day. Time did not pass through Transit without decay. It was a barren place with no markings for day or night. Just time outstretched, refusing to be marked by arrivals or departures. There were no shadows and no light. There were no houses, no shelters, no food. Instinctively, people knew they had survived some terrible ordeal that spat them out into this place. But what had they escaped? What had they run away from? Saleh's memory sieved through the hour glass. The fewer memories he had the older he felt. The only proof he had that he had arrived from a different place were his four children, lying next to him—waiting for something, anything—to happen. He had a wife—he vaguely remembered her. But she never made it to Transit. She must have stayed in Point A. Was she alive? Why hadn't she made it here with them?

When news spread in Transit, it spread like a siren call. The source was invisible and the message demanded action. Like hope roused temporarily only to be abandoned once again.

'They're saying the government of Point B have voted to allow our children to cross.'

'But only a few hundred. Look around you, there are hundreds of thousands of them. How will they choose?'

'Each family has to choose one child who can go. The rest will wait here until another government allows them to cross over.'

Saleh listened to the conversation while he squatted nearby. So he has to choose one of his children to send to Point B on their own, in the hope that this child will someday grow up and be able to help speed the rest of them across the border. If only his wife were here, he thought. She would help him choose. He seemed to remember that she was far more pragmatic than he was.

'Who will you send, Saleh? You know, I wish I didn't look so old. I would've tried to lie my way across the border. I don't pass for 18 anymore, do I?'

Saleh looked at the man who had grown more familiar since he had arrived at Transit. His name was Nizam and he talked a lot; seemed to remember random odds and ends from a previous life. Annoying, monotonous things. Things Saleh could neither understand nor find the sense of humour to acknowledge politely. Transit demanded sobriety. An acceptance of the tragic without protest. There was no point in protesting anything here. Saleh sensed that they deserved to be here; not only because they deserved a second chance after escaping the huge fire in Point A but also because they deserved to be punished for what they had not appreciated while living there. Whatever had happened in Point A, Saleh thought, could not have been worse than what is happening now. And whatever Point B has to offer, it is unlikely to be worth this never-ending wait.

'Give them the beautiful one.'

'Keef yâny? What are you saying?'

'Give them the beautiful one. They like dark kids with green eyes.'

'But I've heard that they are all beautiful and all have green eyes.'

'Yes, they'll think he's one of them.'

But he is not one of them. He is one of us. If he doesn't learn their ways, will they throw him out here again? Saleh stared emptily at the man offering him solutions.

'No, not Yaseen. It'd break his mother's heart.'

'Whomever you give them it will break her heart. Didn't you say she never made it here? She'll never know.'

'What if I give them my daughter Yasmin?'

'Are you mad? Where's your honour! She'll grow up among strangers and sleep with men not of our blood or creed. She'll have many children by different fathers!'

A layer of soot covered Saleh's heart. No, his daughter could stay with him, by his side. Should he die, she would die with him.

But she's a clever girl. What if she goes there and blossoms? But what will my townspeople say? They will make me dangle my head in shame.

'You have a disabled son, no? I hear they take real good care of kids like that over there.'

But how will Waleed bring the rest of them over? He won't be able to make enough money to help them. Choosing him must be a long-term investment.

'I could send Waseem. He's a clever boy. He will grow up in no time and come back to help us.'

'Isn't he your youngest son? He's barely five. It will be decades before he can help you. And your other children will resent you for the rest of your life.'

He suddenly understood the architectural genius behind Transit: the infinite emptiness, the unbearable immeasurability of time, the diminishing of memory and hope... It was the burial ground for human resilience. Perhaps things mattered in Point A. Maybe even had significance and were worth fighting for. Made a difference. Perhaps death was not the worse outcome after all that had happened. And if Transit is where people went to be humiliated to point zero, then what kind of life awaited them at Point B that had to be prepared for in this way? Subjugation? Slavery? What kind of freedom were they offering when they would only allow a parentless child to go through? Don't these children need to stay with their families? And if Point B is the safe haven, why on earth would they want to avoid it? Who would want to avoid it?

He could not remember. And as he spent hours—perhaps days, even months or years—contemplating, he did not realise that he had stopped thinking altogether. He was merely acting like he had thoughts to offer the empty space that surrounded them. He squatted on the yellow marble terrain, staring towards an invisible Point B, wondering if death was really worth running from.

Crossing Borders by

Adrienne Silcock

I have plundered art galleries
shovelled up banks of wild flowers
pulled skeins from loose grey skies
to knit a blanket for your shivering back

I have watched your journey,
or the likes of it, on TV
the rough roads, the squalid camps,
the drownings.

You hunker down your hope
watch clouds unravel
dream of petals that unfurl at home
how you might have painted them

the one thing you wish for is denied
borders are more than frames for pictures
you see no edges in the skies.

Winter Solstice by Penny Simpson

afternoon

In the fading light of a winter solstice day, Maud watches the helium balloon free itself from a tangle of branches. When she was little, she often worried about the legions of balloons that must be adrift in the sky. She imagined birds pecking their skins and dying of heart attacks when they exploded. The worry was that millions of dead birds and fragments of balloons would rain down and smother her, in a downpour of helium-silver feathers. Da sang to calm her: 'Catch a *moonbeam in a jar.*' She knew she would be catching fragments of feathery, silver balloons.

Da said, miracles happen in the blink of an eye. And did she remember Our Lady going on her travels? She remembers him tucking the plaster statue under his arm and taking it down the road to their house when Nana died; sidestepping the kerbstones painted the wrong colours to his way of thinking. The whole tribe of them kicking with the left foot in a street full of strangers. It was the way of it, from the get-go, Maud thinks.

She stands still and fixes her gaze on the balloon, a temporary miracle interrupting the fading of the day. It is dusk. It is cold. Maud pulls the collar of her fur coat up. The coat is from a charity shop and it is a wonder too. She sleeps with it wrapped around her and it is like being snuggled by a bear. It's supposed to be rabbit fur. How many rabbits to make a coat? It could be a line from a song. She hums a melody and tries the line out. The Doherty's were great ones for the singing. A song for every occasion, even stepping out on a winter's afternoon and chasing down the streets for a last ray of sunshine. Maud wonders what song Da would have chosen for her today. It is dusk. It is cold. It is seven months, five days and eighteen hours since she gave up the needle. It is a miracle. It's nearly Christmas, so maybe it's a double miracle. On solstice day, Da mixed glitter with Weetabix for reindeer food. Bitsy bits of silver in the breakfast mush which Maud secretly picked out and ate herself. X-ray the inside of her stomach, and it will be like looking inside a helium balloon. A magical, glittering belly hides under her fur coat, made from the skins of one hundred and one rabbits. For this, she has decided, is the exact number needed to make a fur coat.

It is dusk. It is the winter solstice—the longest night of the year. The nights are already too long for someone who sleeps sporadically. Without the heroin, she has bad dreams. She pinches herself to keep awake and stop the dreams sliding in behind her eyes. Others have bad dreams too. She hears the woman in the flat next door cry out, a petite woman she has occasionally glimpsed on the stairwell by day, memorable because of the colourfully embroidered scarves wound round her head. Maud assumes she comes from somewhere faraway, because of the scarves and the painted arch of her eyebrows and her skin the colour of a manilla envelope. A few days ago, the woman smiled at her.

Maud isn't used to being smiled at and she worries over the gesture. She worries she should have smiled back; she worries she might have to speak to the woman if she smiles at her again. *Smile, and the whole world smiles with you.* Except it is cold. It is dusk. The light ebbs and the world recedes. Passers-by are reduced to silhouettes. Maud holds her lapels between balled fists and closes her eyes. Is it cold enough to snow on the longest night of the year? She listens in to her memory of Da pounding glitter into a bowl of crumbled Weetabix. A smudge of a memory.

evening

Maud opens her eyes. Here is her street, and here is the block of flats where she has lived for nearly three months without once talking to any of her neighbours. Social housing is something of an oxymoron in Aneurin Bevan Street. Maud picks up a small stone. She wants to play hopscotch, but is interrupted by a woman calling out:

'Do you see them?'

She looks up and there is her neighbour, standing on a second floor balcony. Her headscarf has worked loose, and her hair cuts across her face.

'The assassinators try and kill me. Come up, please.'

Maud hears the fear in her voice and heads for the stairwell. The woman is waiting for her when she reaches the top of the stairs. She has adjusted her headscarf and donned a man's overcoat. The belt buckle taps along behind her as she ushers Maud into her apartment and out on to the balcony. They stand side by side and inspect a heap of broken plant pots.

'Whoosh! And down they come. Nearly take my head off. I call the police.' The woman claims the pots have been dropped by the couple who live above her. 'They hate me because I am foreigner.'

'I'm not from here, either.'

'That's what I think.'

Maud tries to think of an excuse to leave, but the woman is offering her tea. She looks exhausted, as if she has been waiting for days to accost a passer-by to stand witness.

Maud relents and returns to the living room. Its dimensions mirror her own, but there the comparison ends, for her neighbour is house proud. The sofa is swathed in a richly embroidered cloth, pierced with tiny fragments of mirror; dried flowers are arranged in vases on the windowsill and the low-slung coffee table. There is the scent of something unfamiliar, maybe a spice, or the woman's perfume. Maud takes a seat on the sofa. When the police turn up, she remains seated. One of the officers yawns and doesn't try to hide her indifference; the other scribbles in his notebook, before delivering his verdict.

'Let's be clear, Mrs Mojaradi. If you decide this is a racist attack, you'll be opening a can of worms. Are you really prepared to go to court?'

Mrs Mojaradi embarks on another explanation. She tells the policeman she is from Persia, but he will probably know it as Iran. In Persia-Iran, there is no rule of law but she understands that there is in the UK. Maud feels sorry for her neighbour. She is out of her depth. It is a state of being very familiar to Maud.

'Mrs Mojaradi has confirmed she is happy to go to court and give evidence.'

'But I'm not happy, lovely. And who might you be?'

Maud has had many aliases over the years, but none seem quite right to meet the circumstances. The woman officer circles her.

'You're known to me, aren't you, Maud?'

Mrs Mojaradi frowns, before light dawns. She claps her hands in the air, as if catching at moths.

'It is a miracle, they know you!'

'It's not that sort of knowing someone.'

Maud feels she's let Mrs Mojaradi down. The policewoman knows her, because the police always know people like Maud. She is embarrassed to have her neighbour know about this kind of knowing. She often lets people down, but today she wanted to do things differently, because she's been off the needle far longer than she could ever have hoped for, and it's a solstice miracle. The police leave without much more being said or done. Mrs Mojaradi tugs at her sleeve.

'Tonight, I hold a party for an angel. At seven o'clock. Will you come?'

She opens her arms wide and turns round on the spot, like a circus ringmaster. Maud sees the room is as dingy as her own under its drapes and the scent of spicy flowers; the plaster on the ceiling is cracked and the wall-mounted gas fire is surrounded by scorch marks. What angel would hold a party in such a room? Maud hugs her coat to her. An angel's party. It is, she realises, exactly the kind of miracle to hope for on a winter's solstice night. Da wouldn't have turned a hair. Hadn't he criss-crossed the street with our Lady tucked up under his arm for safe-keeping? He made reindeer food and sang the world into submission. He never once carried a gun, not like other men.

'What's the birthday angel called, Mrs Mojaradi?'

'It is Mithra. And, please, wear something green.'

Maud's excitement disintegrates the minute she leaves the apartment and enters her own. Her cupboards are bare, the floorboards barer still. No potted plant or luxury box of chocolates, not even a chocolate button. She returns to the landing and knocks on her neighbour's door.

'I don't have anything to bring, Mrs Mojaradi, so I'd rather not impose.'

Mrs Mojaradi doesn't seem to get the picture. Maud tries to think of another way of saying: I have nothing. Her neighbour smiles.

'You bring you.'

She shuts the door, leaving Maud standing on the welcome mat in a state of some confusion. Parties mean gifts, bottles of booze and homemade quiche, and egg-and-cress sandwiches, and rows of chocolate fingers banked up on the best plates, and paper serviettes, and Da at the piano, singing into the wee hours. Maybe Mithra does things differently, because he's Persian and he's an angel? She knows she's forgotten a lot more than party etiquette; she's forgotten how to speak, how to smile. She's forgotten because she's had to; she's forgotten because of going on the needle; she's forgotten because when she was six years old our Lady got blown up and Da with her. They burst into pieces like the helium balloons which kill the birds and make silver rain. It is winter solstice. It is cold.

night

This is what Maud thinks: she'll wear her green chiffon blouse over the camisole that hasn't got torn yet. She'll wipe her biker boots and get the last smear of lipstick off the tube with a cotton bud. She is going to party with angels. When her neighbour opens her door, Maud thinks she's an angel too. She wears a peacock blue dress; her lips are red and her eyes heavily kohl-ed. She hugs Maud, tighter than tight, and it's a shock because no one has held her like this for a very long time. Mrs Mojaradi explains it is Yalda, the Persian winter solstice. It is Mithra's birthday and Mithra is the angel of light and truth. In Persia, there are parties and celebrations held in his honour. And there are pomegranates, although Maud has no idea what a pomegranate is. Mrs Mojaradi signals for her coat. As she pulls it off, the blouse she wears unbuttoned over her camisole slips away. Mrs Mojaradi gently circles the usually hidden-away skin with her fingertips.

'Join-the-dots.'

Maud freezes. She can't remember what it is she should do or say when someone behaves like this, when someone is being kind. Da said, with genuine people there are no strings. They are not like the Big Men with their judgements and general hully-balloo. Mrs Mojaradi shows her a faded snapshot of a young woman.

'It is my daughter Khina,' she says. 'When the Green Revolution starts, she was a student of literature. They paint their hands green for the victory. But she is arrested and they torture her. Twenty two years old. They kill her. No trial.'

Mrs Mojaradi and Maud sit side by side, the snapshot suspended between them, each holding a corner. It is a reliquary, like the one Mam made for her when she came to study at art college, three prayer medals and a tiny crucifix stitched into a little felt and leather wallet. It has been lost, like green-handed Khina.

'Mrs Mojaradi...'

'My name is Azarin. It means chamomile.'

'And Maud means powerful battler. Like a warrior.'

'I have the same name as a Persian princess who was a military general. So, we are both warriors.'

Maud remembers a description in her school history book of a meeting between warrior kings on the Field of the Cloth of Gold. The tents were woven out of real gold filament, the sort she imagines lining a Persian desert, but really she has no idea what a desert is like, or a Green Revolution, or a princess-general. But she learns what a pomegranate is, because Azarin shows her how to open one with a little silver knife. She places her hand over Maud's and they circle the top of the fruit, revealing the segments beneath. They make eight vertical cuts following the lines of the segments and prise the fruit open. Azarin uses the pomegranates to make a soup called *Āsh-e ānar*. As she cooks, she tells stories about life back home.

It is a place Maud recognises, for back home is where Da walked with our Lady and Mam stitched reliquaries to watch over her faraway children. There, Da stood, beneath the Union Jack flags which hung from the neighbours' windows. He refused to go into exile, or even move behind a wall of barbed wire. He said: 'Here's where I was born; here's where I plant my flag,' except it wasn't a flag, but a statue of our Lady. He planted her in the garden, just under Maud's bedroom window. 'When you wake up, you'll think you're in Heaven.'

'Tonight, back home, everyone reads poetry,' Azarin says.

'Will you read for me? Hafez is my country's greatest poet. I find him on the Internet in the library.'

Maud feels awkward. She's never been a great reader-out. Azarin takes a piece of paper from her handbag.

'Please. I want to hear the English words.'

Maud takes the paper and reads:

'*A message has arrived to say that the days of sorrow will not last.*
What happened in the past did not last for ever.
And nor will what is in the present last for ever either.'

daybreak

The cusp of a new day; Maud sits inside a magic circle conjured out of word and flame, recalling an angel and a lost child with green hands. Azarin is curled up on the sofa beside her, in a deep sleep. When it gets lighter, Maud blows out the Yalda candles. She criss-crosses the room on bare feet, accompanied by the hiss of the radiator. Slipping on her coat, she makes a decision, the first in a long while. When Azarin wakes, she'll accompany her to the police station and, together, they'll file her complaint.

You, Sameh by Kathy Stevens

In your own country, you were training to be a nurse. I suppose that's the first thing that stuck out to me, one of the factors that made me choose you over the hundreds of others, because when I was your age, I was training to be a nurse too. I felt guilty for choosing you, because it meant that I was rejecting all the other people who needed help. It felt slightly worse than not helping anyone at all, at first. I didn't like feeling so omnipotent, but it would've been worse to let the agency choose someone and for us to have nothing to talk about, because I wouldn't have had the heart to terminate the agreement. So I chose you, and asked you if you'd like to come to work with me. I was happy when you agreed straight away.

I felt bad about giving you 12 hour shifts, like the others, and not being able to pay you for your work, but you said, in your broken English, that the use of my spare room was payment enough. You never once complained... you worked harder than any of the other care assistants, getting your

hands dirty and doing the jobs that nobody else wanted to
do. You said you were so grateful to work, even long hours
for no money, and you said it with such open enthusiasm that
I wondered if you knew what 'grateful' meant, I wondered if
you had mistaken it for another word.

I was worried about the staff taking advantage of you, but
you won them over quickly. Soon they were greeting you
at the start of each shift with cheery calls of 'I-hilen' and
'kaytha-hilicha' and you would ask at break times 'fancy a
brew?' in your developing northern accent. You were a bit
like a mascot to them, and to the home, and I hoped you
wouldn't feel demeaned; you never showed it, if you were. I
was there for almost a year before a handful of them began
to respect me; you were there a week and already they were
asking you out to the pub. This was a problem I hadn't
anticipated. When you knocked on my office door as I was
eating my sandwich one afternoon, I said 'come,' and seeing
it was you, I gestured to an empty chair. You didn't speak for
such a long time that I had swallowed my mouthful and taken
another bite. Then you began to cry, and it was the first time
you had cried in front of me, though I'd heard you sometimes
very late at night through the wall of the spare room.

'It is difficult,' you said, and I nodded for you to continue,
but you couldn't find the words. This surprised me, because
your English was getting very good.

'It is a stupid thing. No big problem, but I don't know how
to do.'

'Is someone giving you a hard time?' I asked.

'No, nothing like that. Everyone is so nice, too nice to me
really.'

'I'll try to help if I can...' I gave you a tissue and you dabbed
your eyes.

'The staff, they have invite me for drinking with them after work. And it is a wonderful thing, but not possible for me.'

I understood what you meant. You had no clothes other than a couple of government issued t-shirts and the carer's uniform I'd provided you with, and your faith didn't allow you to drink alcohol. You were given only five pounds per day by the government for food and travel, and though I had tried to give you money before, just a few coins to rattle in your pocket, you had always refused with a shy smile.

'I don't know how to make them understand, I am not only poor. They are poor, earning so small money and working much hours every week, but I am poorer still. I am not complaint! I am very grateful to live here and have wonderful job looking after old people. I make many good friends, but I cannot be like them. I am sorry to cry.' You looked very sorry too, your eyes were barely meeting mine. It seemed as though you were ashamed by your unhappiness, as though you didn't have the right to be unhappy when people from your country were worse off than you.

'Then we'll throw a party, at mine.' I said, then changed my mind 'At ours.'

You shook your head rapidly back and forth, dried your tears on the back of your olive hand.

'No, is not any big problem. I am sorry, I didn't mean to ask you anything.'

'Friday night, 7 o'clock, it's settled. You'll give me a list of the ingredients you need, and I'll buy them. You can cook one of your meals that your mother taught you, and invite the shift from work. No arguments.'

'You are a most wonderful person. I want to thank you for your kindness but I cannot, when I have nothing. One day I shall have a good job and money of my own. I'll pay you then for all you have done.'

'There's no need.' I said, reddening 'I've been meaning to throw a party for a long time anyway.' This was not strictly true, I had nothing in common with my employees, and little desire to get to know them, but I knew it was the only way you would agree. I didn't like it when you called me 'wonderful', because I took you in to make *myself* feel better, because *I* was lonely, because I simply could. So, your welfare, even at the point of welcoming you into my home, came second to mine. I wouldn't take a man, even though they were the last to be housed. I wouldn't take a family because I didn't want to have to make the room. I took you, an educated girl of 22, because you were the easiest option for me, and because having you come to live with me was less painful than being alone. So, you see, I am not wonderful, I am really quite selfish. You left the office with another of your shy smiles, and by the end of the shift, we had four confirmed guests for our dinner party.

Michelle was the first to arrive. She's probably your closest friend in England. Being a couple of years younger and without much education, it's a smaller gap to bridge, yours and hers. I know a lot about her, as I've access to her personal files. She came from a care background, hopping from one kid's home to another and routinely written off by her new teachers. They say that each time a child moves school, their education is set back by six months – that'd make Michelle about 12. She looks up to you, and I know you don't notice it but I do. She copies your mannerisms, the way you always pull your shoulders back when you walk, and the small clips that keep your hair smooth against your scull. With her fair hair and pale freckly skin, she looks like a ghost of you when she follows you around. You like her very much, she often makes you laugh. You don't see what she's doing, and you wouldn't believe me if I told you; you would never believe that someone from England would aspire to be like you. When she arrived, I held out my hand and she shook it roughly on the doorstep. Inside, I offered her a glass of wine, and she grasped it by the bowl, not taking a sip. Neither of us really knew what to say or how to be with each other, so she followed the smell of garlic into the kitchen where you were preparing dinner, and a moment later I heard the sound of you both laughing. I wondered what you were talking about in there, but I felt sure that she wouldn't speak freely in front of me so I rearranged the cushions on the sofa, and rubbed at a water-mark on one of the knives set for dinner.

I was relieved when I answered the second doorbell to find that last three guests had arrived together, and by the look of them, they'd already had a glass or two. The conversation flowed quite freely in the living room. There was a moment of awkwardness when I offered the wine, and they each requested beer. But I found, to my relief, a half-full crate of lager belonging to my ex-husband in the garage. It had only just gone past its date, so I wiped off the dust with a tea-towel and decanted it into high-ball glasses as they watched.

We spoke about work, the four of us, for a while, me staying mostly silent, and them swapping glances before each new observation, mutually deciding what was and was not appropriate to say in front of the boss. Then they asked me about you – I answered their questions about the community hosting programme frankly, and they replied with polite nods. It seemed wrong to pry into your life when you were still out of earshot with Michelle in the kitchen, so only the most neutral, non-committal comments could be made. It also felt wrong to discuss your country, or Islam, and besides, I suspected that they didn't know enough about those subjects to sustain a long discourse. The conversation was floundering, and when you let out another of your throaty, musical laughs, we craned as one in your direction, hopeful that you might emerge and break the tension.

Just when Margaret, the aging housekeeper, had got stiffly up from my sofa, and was making a beeline for the smiling photos of my dead marriage on the mantel, I was saved by your emergence from the kitchen. You were holding my casserole dish, which looked strange, full as it was of your national dish, *fatteh*. Bill, the maintenance man, stood up and clapped, and after a moment's hesitation, Margaret and then Sandra, the fat duty nurse, joined in. I didn't clap, but I smiled at you and you returned the expression before laying the dish carefully in the centre of the dining table.

'Tuck in!' you said, and everyone kissed your cheeks before taking their seat. Some of them kissed Michelle too, or grasped her hand in something between an embrace and a handshake. Nobody kissed or touched me, and I stood a little back from you all, like an anti-social family pet, hoping for a scrap from the table I hadn't been invited to dine at.

'Before we eat, I would like to do a toast for Joanne,' you said, when everyone was settled.

'It's not necessary,' I said, 'really it isn't.' But you were already standing, with your glass of orange-juice raised high. Bill stood up too, hoisting his out-of-date lager. The others just sat up a little straighter.

'We will all have a drink about the kindest lady I have ever met,' you said.

'...Ever met,' repeated the others, and we began to eat.

'This is bloody lovely!' said Bill after a few moments, 'Is this Halal then?'

'Um, no. There is no animal in the food. It is made with chick-peas and yoghurt, bread and spices.'

'And garlic by the smell of it, phwoar! Good job we're *all* eating it is all I can say!' They laughed at this.

I was surprised to note that Sandra was picking bits out of the sauce and wiping them on the edge of her plate with her knife.

'I can heat you up some macaroni cheese, if you don't like it.' I said, immediately regretting it. The table went very quiet and all I could hear was Bill's messy eating.

'No, it's very nice.' said Sandra.

'So,' said Margaret, helping herself to one of the beers I'd left on the table and drinking it from the can, 'where's your husband this evening, Joanne?'

'He left me six months ago.' I said. It was the first time I had voiced this to anyone other than my mother, who had Alzheimer's. I can say anything to her and know she'll have forgotten by the next day.

'Oh, God I'm sorry. I've put my foot in it.'

'No, it's OK. He didn't like the hours I was doing. And...' *I've come this far,* I thought, 'and he wanted a child, and I didn't. Didn't have the time.' I finished, and, to my shame, burst into tears.

Margaret was the first out of her seat, then you and Sandra got up too and you all put your arms around me. For a very long time we stayed like that, me sobbing into Margaret's chest, and Sandra and you patting every other part of me.

'Why didn't you say, girl?' said Bill, who looked over warmly but hadn't been able to drag himself from your *fatteh*.

'I-I didn't want to seem w–weak.' He handed me his napkin and said, 'It's better to admit to being a bit vulnerable sometimes, than be a complete bitch all of the time.' He said it very warmly, as though it was perfectly normal to call your hostess a bitch.

'She is not bitch!' you cried. 'She is most wonderful person I ever know!' and you put your arms protectively around me, which were soft and smelt faintly of garlic. After a while, I gently removed your arms and everyone resumed their seats. Nobody ate apart from Bill, who hadn't stopped.

'I am a bitch.' I said. Bill nodded very slightly. Michelle looked intensely at her chickpeas. The two older women turned to me in mild interest, Sandra placing her chin on her bent index finger in a surprisingly graceful gesture.

'I wasn't always, but I have been for a long time. Because of my husband... because of my marriage falling apart. I couldn't tell anyone, I didn't have anyone to tell. I only took Sameh in because I was lonely!'

The table was very quiet, even Bill had stopped eating.

To everyone's surprise, Michelle spoke. 'Well, isn't that why anyone does anything?' You nodded, and so did Margaret.

'I don't think you're a bitch.' said Sandra, 'Maybe a bit firm, but not a bitch.'

'Thank you.'

Everyone looked to Bill, who had turned back to his plate and was busy wiping a piece of pitta round it. You said his name.

'What?' he looked at you, frowning, 'Oh, I don't know! Get us another drink and I'll have a think about it,' he said, and winked, and I could tell it would be all right. You smiled at me, and went into our kitchen to get some more beer.

Nina and the Rain by Kenneth Stevens

Everyone is waiting—

Waiting in Koolambalor, Zbamba and Dar es Malay.

Nina and her mother are waiting in their little house

And there isn't a sound, outside or in.

Nina is sitting with her elbows on the windowsill

Looking at the blue, blue sky

Wishing and wishing that the rain would come.

Everything is thirsty

In Koolambalor, Zbamba and Dar es Malay,

And the river is thin as a snake and slides

Slow and silent to the sea.

At night Nina creeps to her bedroom window,

She can see the stars bright in the sky,

Little eyes watching her.

They are like crocodiles in the lake,

Their yellow eyes watching.

Nina holds her breath and listens

But there isn't so much as a sound.

Then, just before morning,

She wakens and listens to a tapping on the roof.

Is it something else, an insect or a bird?

Then another tap, and another, just fingertips—

But Nina is sure, she lies listening

To the sound of the new rain.

It's a song in the early morning

And Nina rushes to the window,

She throws open the curtains and opens the glass,

And shouts to her mum, 'The rain's come at last!'

And in Koolambalor, Zbamba and Dar es Malay

They rush to their windows and open them wide,

They shout and they sing together

For the rain has come at last.

And Nina and Nina's mum hurry

They go out through the streets

That are busy with everyone else.

They go out into the rain

That's singing from the steeples

And singing from the rooftops

And singing from the stones.

Nina and her mum

Get on a bus

To go far out into the country

To watch the rain falling.

For when it rains

On Koolambalor, Zbamba and Dar es Malay

The storks shriek and gather like clouds at the swamp,

The zebras stamp and shake their manes.

And the buses that drive from the city

To Koolambalor, Zbamba and Dar es Malay—

They crash through the pools, they swish through the mud,

Let the chocolate water swim across their windscreens,

Swirl their wheels. They roar and race

Out over the city streets to the wild, big country,

To the warm rains, the silky soft rain

Of Koolambalor, Zbamba and Dar es Malay.

And Nina is happy at last.

The Border by Susannah Tassell

The child brushed tears from his father's face,

His grubby hands moth soft.

Please don't cry father, please don't cry,

You are brave father, so brave.

I am broken son, so broken.

There is no way forward.

There is no way back.

The child embraced his father's neck,

His small, tired arms, stick thick.

You kept me safe on the wild, wild sea,

You are strong father, so strong.

I am scared son, so scared.

There is no way forward.

There is no way back.

The child gazed into his father's eyes;

You carried me high on the stone-strewn road,

You said we would walk to a better life.

Were you wrong father? Were you wrong?

Our dreams are dust son,

All dust. Nobody wants us.

Nobody.

There is no way forward.

There is no way back.

Émigré by Anna Vaught

I was far from home. I stood on the grey street corner.

I was far from home and stood at the mouth of the sea, ivory curls around my feet.

I was far from home. I stood outside the stores and restaurants at night;

sat in the hotel room, the train compartment, the gimcrack coffee shop;

watched the dark frontiers fade out as the yellow jack of the gas station made midday;

I traced the sad cars on the motorway and my eyes hurt from the strip light.

Memory seared and I drank sour coffee and ate a chocolate bar.

I was far from home; an outsider—tossed up as motes from some former life, composed of Eros, intellect, memory and uncertain dust.

But I was you and I was me. Everyman; foreigner; flâneur; such longueur: étranger—

And did you care? Did you stare? But did you know?

We are all from an island or a foreign sun and every one of us uncertain; alone—

the human condition isolates us; our experience, our very world

blunted by language of a raggedy drum, our faith sharp and clear

or not so, as we cry out our unbelief, our refugee song,

but together. We beat our palms against the past, each a piece of the continent,

a part of the main: our love tremulous in our hands, like water that shall spill.

The Candidate by Elisa Marcella Webb

The black Lexus purred under the magnolia trees. The driver, a candidate, leaned forward to check the house number. Yep, the right house. Big, but not ostentatious. Old money, no need to advertise. He had a photo of his late Mama and Daddy outside a house just like this one. Different State, same story. Mama in an apron, Daddy in overalls, both laughing, fit to burst. It was summer of '71, '72? They'd got engaged that week. Heading out after work, up to Dexter Avenue Baptist, ask the pastor if he'd do them the honour of marrying them. Mama and Daddy trying to look solemn, pulling on their church faces. Boss's son wanted Kodak's. Black and white photos of coloured folk were all the rage back then. But Mama and Daddy were so happy they laughed, the kid snapped, the picture took. Daddy laid down four dollars for a print.

The candidate stepped out of the cool Lexus into the rippling heat. It rolled down the street like a new tide. He swung his jacket over his shoulder. Then thought better of it and dumped the jacket back on the seat. On the curb, two guys, one much older than the other, were sweating over some kegs.

'Hey,' they said, then almost stood to attention, their brown skin beaded with sweat. They recognised him. The candidate felt bashful, as usual. He wondered, prayed, he wouldn't lose this. Humility, his pastor called it.

'Hey,' he replied and walked over for some chat, shoot the breeze. The candidate did his thing: leaning in, head down, nodding. While he listened to their gripes and hopes, a white woman opened the screen door. She hallooed: 'Boys, *oh boys*.' The edge in her voice: like grit in your eye. 'Y'all can take that round the back, poolside.' She smiled like she was giving out favours. The 'boys' cut their eyes, pissed. The candidate knew this wasn't the first or last little humiliation that make up a man's life. The woman remained stiff at the door, frowning, impatient. The help were making the lawn untidy.

'Com'on,' the elder man bent his greying head over the keg. His collar sweat stained, his back braced against the sun's weight. The candidate rolled up his $500-shirt-sleeves and bent too. And together the three black men laboured around the porch, out across the vast back lawn. The younger man started to whistle, the elder took up the chorus in a deep baritone. It was the candidate's campaign song; the men glanced across the keg, letting the candidate know *he* didn't have to join in unless *he* really knew the words. He did. United they marched poolside.

The guests reacted in confusion, moving aside, pulling chairs apart; though they were yards away. Children stared, a dog barked. They dropped the keg as the crowd started to clap; iced beers were thrust at their hands; backs were slapped. A senator asked the old man about his route, three pony-tailed girls surrounded the younger man. He glanced across at the candidate, bashful. So this is what victory feels like, the candidate thought and smiled.

The Calais Jungle by Ian Shaw

At the time of writing, there are over 200 unaccompanied kids from Civil War zones, with family in the UK, stranded on a toxic wasteland, 23 miles from our coast.

I have been working for a year now as a volunteer at the unofficial refugee camp—known as the *jungle*—in Calais, France.

I began by taking a mountain of food, clothes and musical instruments, kindly donated by friends and fans. The response was overwhelming. My jazz and comedy community came forward. Julian Clary donated and made dinner for singer Polly Gibbons and me on the eve of our first trip. Actors, broadcasters, producers, neighbours, family, bar managers, shopkeepers, football agents. My funny old world sat up and listened. My funny old world acted. The fundraising gigs began. More and more of my community started coming out to help. To the *jungle*—a lawless, yet often stimulating microcosm of all our funny old worlds.

This is not my story. I was just a tiny cog in a huge wheel

that simply does not turn fast enough. I began to form firm friendships with vulnerable, dignified, hugely compromised people—and gradually, over many teas I heard only horrific stories. Stories of vile, seemingly never-ending journeys—one young mother of 23 finally having the courage to tell singer and volunteer Georgia Mancio and me that her sister and two year old daughter simply fell out the boat. As the winter kicked in, my determination to continue was undimmed. You cannot 'unsee' stuff. I witnessed solvable problems being unsolved. Pointless and upsetting brutality from riot police. Refugees would call me at 3am, desperately needing my car to take yet another group of badly injured minors to A&E in Calais. This and the constant attacks on distressed young refugees from the far right groups around the camp.

And utter, sheer compassion. Actress Juliet Stevenson bought a bus for the kids, after the horror of a demolition so brutal and futile, it beggared belief that there was any humanity left. Actor Jude Law visited. The extraordinary Good Chance Theatre provided a sanctuary and stimulation for bored, dissolute damaged young people. There was hope and there was hopelessness. The domed theatre was dismantled before the local authorities could destroy it, with as much cold dispassion as they'd poured on the shocking razing of a tarpaulin mosque and a church.

As NGOs and unregistered small grass-root groups extended collective arms of protection around the camp, I kept bumping into one young woman. Sometimes in the lobby of our accommodation, but often in the mud and sludge of the camp. She is Laura Griffiths. I doubt I will ever meet a braver, more determined, brighter soul in my life. Her brief is to compile and process humanely, via Citizens

UK and Safe Passage, a full list of the unaccompanied kids I mentioned at the beginning. The only way she can do this is to gain the love and confidence of these distressed kids. She is in the camp most days, sensitively and with affection and much laughter, along with a small team of trusted co-workers from Safe Passage, collecting details which when processed will allow a judiciary review.

I was invited by George at Citizens UK to speak at a memorial celebrating the life of a 15 year old whose existence in *the jungle* had got the better of him. He died trying to escape.

The following two days, Laura and her team won a case—Minor's Human Rights versus The Home Office. A process began legally allowing minors' cases one by one, letting these vulnerable children be reunified, under the Dublin III Regulation, in the UK—currently a European member state.

However, in recent months, we have seen a slowing down of this process. Labour MP Stella Creasy recently travelled to join Side By Side Refugees (I'm a trustee and media spokesperson for this UK charity) in *the jungle*. It was a good day. Amber Rudd, Home Secretary, has been invited. Is it not a huge, moral and fair duty, for Rudd to witness the truth of the crisis? And not rely on third-hand, biased reports? Creasy is clear, pragmatic and compassionate—and met a lot of *jungle* residents. Side By Side and I made sure of this.

Laura Griffiths will continue her painstaking work. With no governmental support. The money raised is a drop in this unforgivably deep and wide ocean. But without funds, this work will be massively compromised. Please support her and Citizens UK/Safe Passage. We cannot let this untenable cruelty define our next generation.

In Canada 31,000 Syrian refugees have been welcomed. 'What matters is that we learn from our mistakes' said Justin Trudeau, adding: it's been a 'long-overdue welcome.'

But Teresa May and Amber Rudd ignore our pleas to create a vital humanitarian initiative here in the UK. In the shrivelled, sour, cold and heartless soul in our country, with an economy that is statistically, without argument, MORE than well-equipped to assimilate people who ACTUALLY want to work—we cannot even consider the plight of a few hundred unaccompanied kids, with UK family connections. These are kids whose cases are being built, via the Dublin III Regulation—by the extraordinary above-mentioned Laura, Citizens UK/Safe Passage —ASIDE from the '3,000' whose safe passage was promised via the Dubs Amendment, in The House, in the early spring—with zilch follow-up. Amber Rudd has ignored our pleas, via the Home Office, to create a vital humanitarian initiative here. It continues. It is pathetic.

Our government's inaction on this will historically expose the UK as the shrunken, isolationist island it has politically become.

To place vulnerable young people's lives at risk, so close to our shore, is beyond brutal.

Refugee Charities

Auberge des Migrants

http://www.laubergedesmigrants.fr

Citizens UK

http://www.citizensuk.org

The Compassionate Collective

http://thecompassioncollective.org

Crisis Action

https://crisisaction.org

Help Refugees

http://www.helprefugees.org.uk

Human Rights Watch

https://www.hrw.org

Or Hope not Hate

http://www.hopenothate.org.uk

Red Cross

http://www.redcross.org.uk

Refugee Action

http://www.refugee-action.org.uk

Refugee Council

https://www.refugeecouncil.org.uk

Safe Passage

www.safepassage.org.uk

Side by Side Refugees

https://sidebysiderefugees.org

UNHRC The UN Refugee Agency

http://www.unhcr.org/uk

Unicef UK

http://www.unicef.org.uk

White Helmets

https://www.whitehelmets.org

Contributor details

Anna Johnson is a children's book editor.
anna@patricianpress.com

Pen Avey is a UK-based writer and illustrator.
http://www.henandink.com/coop/pavey

Rebecca Balfourth lives in London.
balfourthrb.wordpress.com

Wersha Bharadwa is a journalist and writer.
www.facebook.com/WershasWorld; @wersha

Katherine Blessan is a writer and Creative Writing Tutor.
www.katherineblessan.com; @kathblessan

Mark Brayley is a performance poet living in Colchester.
www.Markbrayley.com

Catherine Coldstream is studying for a PhD
at London, Goldsmiths. www.catherinecoldstream.com

Louise G. Cole lives in County Roscommon, Ireland.
https://louisegcolewriter.wordpress.com/

Priya Guns, educator and founder of Capokolam.
www.priyaguns.net

Naomi Hamill is a writer living in Manchester.
naohamill@hotmail.com; @naohamill

Emma Kittle-Pey is studying for a PhD in Creative Writing
at Essex. @ekittl; @Colwritenight

Aoife Lyall is a teacher and poet living in Inverness,
Scotland. aoifelyall.wordpress.com

Petra McQueen is a writer and teacher living in Wivenhoe.
petramcqueen@gmail.com; @PetraMcQueen

Suzy Norman is a writer and actor living in London.
norman.suzy@gmail.com; @suzynorman

Susan Pope is a novelist and leads the Medway Mermaids
women's writing group in Kent. www.susan-pope.co.uk

Robert Ronsson is a novelist living in Bewdley.
http://robertronsson.co.uk/

Nesreen Salem, writer, feminist, researcher.
nesreen@me.com; @nesreenmsalem

Adrienne Silcock lives in North Yorkshire.
www.adriennesilcock.co.uk

Penny Simpson is a novelist and short story writer.
www.pennysimpson.com; @topscribe

Kathy Stevens is studying for an MA in creative writing at UEA. kathystevenswriter@gmail.com

Kenneth Stevens is a writer living in Dunkeld, Scotland. http://kennethsteven.co.uk

Susannah Tassell lives in Bradford on Avon. susie_freeman@hotmail.com

Anna Vaught is a writer living in Bradford on Avon. www.annavaughtwrites.com

Elisa Marcella Webb is studying for a PhD in Creative Writing at Kingston. elisa.webb101@gmail.com

Ian Shaw, jazz musician. www.ianshaw.biz

Further Reading

No Place for Children report

http://reliefweb.int/report/syrian-arab-republic/no-place-children-impact-five-years-war-syrias-children-and-their

The Guardian

https://www.theguardian.com/world/refugees

https://www.theguardian.com/world/calais

Hassiba Hadj-Sahraoui

https://www.theguardian.com/careers/2016/aug/22/rescuing-refugees-you-never-get-used-to-it-and-thats-a-good-thing

Kate Lyons

https://www.theguardian.com/world/2016/jul/28/from-the-cold-war-to-syria-seven-decades-of-refugee-stories-in-britain

Chimamanda Ngozi-Adichies

http://qz.com/766267/nobody-is-ever-just-a-refugee-chimamanda-ngozi-adichies-powerful-speech-on-the-global-migrant-crisis

http://www.ibtimes.co.uk/britains-hard-hearted-response-calais-kids-destroying-values-that-make-our-country-great-1588392

https://static.independent.co.uk/s3fs-public/styles/story_medium/public/thumbnails/image/2016/10/29/22/photo-2-alan-schaller.jpg

Refugee Tales

http://refugeetales.org

Cargo by Tess Berry-Hart

A Country of Refuge – An Anthology of Writing on Asylum Seekers edited by Lucy Popescu

Who are Refugees and Migrants? What Makes People Leave their Homes? And Other Big Questions by Michael Rosen and Annemarie Young

Publisher's note by Patricia Borlenghi

The idea for the writing competition was conceived at the end of 2015 as I was walking along the Stour Estuary close to my home. I was becoming increasingly frustrated with the failure to stop the war in Syria and the perpetual refugee crisis. Our political leaders seem intent on warmongering rather than pursuing peace. As a very small publisher, I felt helpless and that my only outlet was the pen.

I was delighted with the response to the writing competition and am very proud of the anthology we have published. As well as other invited contributors, it includes the short-listed poems and short stories by Pen Avey, Rebecca Balfourth, Katherine Blessan, Louise G. Cole, Catherine Coldstream, Priya Guns, Aoife Lyall, Susan Pope, Adrienne Silcock and Susannah Tassell. The overall prize winners were Penny Simpson, Kathy Stevens and Naomi Hamill.

Special thanks to Joceline Bury, our 'external' judge, and Anna Johnson, Emma Kittle-Pey and Petra McQueen.